HOLT 1 GERMAN

Komm mit!®

Video Guide

HOLT, RINEHART AND WINSTON

A Harcourt Classroom Education Company

Austin • New York • Orlando • Atlanta • San Francisco • Boston • Dallas • Toronto • London

Contributing Writers

Teacher Suggestions
Patricia Callahan

Student Activities Scripts
Frank Dietz

Copyright © by Holt, Rinehart and Winston

All rights reserved. No part of this publication may be reproduced or transmitted in any form or by any means, electronic or mechanical, including photocopy, recording, or any information storage and retrieval system, without permission in writing from the publisher.

Teachers using KOMM MIT! may photocopy blackline masters in complete pages in sufficient quantities for classroom use only and not for resale.

Cover Photo/Illustration Credits:
Group of students: George Winkler/HRW Photo; videocassette: Image Copyright ©2003 Photodisc, Inc.

KOMM MIT! is a trademark licensed to Holt, Rinehart and Winston, registered in the United States of America and/or other jurisdictions.

Printed in the United States of America

ISBN 0-03-065889-6

4 5 6 7 018 07 06 05

To the Teacher

Komm mit! allows you to integrate video into instruction. The program was shot entirely on location in German-speaking countries and supplies linguistically authentic and culturally rich video support for **Komm mit!**

The *Video Program* provides the following video support for each chapter of the *Pupil's Edition*:

- A narrated **Location Opener** introduces students to each of the four regions explored in the *Pupil's Edition*. This guided tour of the area in which the subsequent three chapters take place expands students' knowledge of the geography, culture, and people of that area.

- The **Los geht's!** section of each chapter is enacted on video. The scripted, controlled language supported by visual cues provides comprehensible input that models the targeted functional expressions, vocabulary, and grammar. This section can be used to present material in the chapter for the first time, to reinforce it as you go through the chapter, and to review it at the end of a lesson cycle.

- The stories presented in the **Los geht's!** section of each chapter are continued in a **Fortsetzung** that brings closure to the dramatic episode. This expanded story allows for additional modeling of targeted functions, vocabulary, and grammar, as well as recycling of previously learned material.

- German captions for every **Los geht's!** and **Fortsetzung** episode are available on Videocassette 5. Target-language captions give students another opportunity to understand the language used in the story and offer you further possibilities for presenting the new material in class. For example, you might play a short segment of the video, rewind and replay it without sound, and then ask students to read the captions aloud or point out familiar words and phrases.

- The **Landeskunde** section presents videotaped interviews with the native speakers of German introduced on the **Landeskunde** page in the *Pupil's Edition*. The unscripted language spoken at a normal rate of speed will give students a taste of "real" German. Teaching suggestions and activity masters in this guide will help students focus on the pertinent information and make the language accessible to them.

- The **Landeskunde** section is expanded with several additional interviews. These additional interviews expose students to a wide range of German speakers and introduce them to several regional accents. The additional opinions and reactions to the topics being discussed give students increased insight into German culture. These are unedited interviews with real people who are using "real," everyday language. Teaching suggestions and activity masters in this guide will help students focus on the pertinent information and make the language accessible to them.

- A special **Videoclips** section provides authentic television footage related to the chapter theme including commercials, weather reports, and music videos. This authentic slice of German television gives students an opportunity to hear and enjoy material produced for native speakers of German and not specifically designed for language learners. While carefully selected to meet pedagogical objectives, in order to preserve authenticity this material was not edited for the classroom. The **Videoclips** should be previewed by teachers before classroom use to ensure the material is appropriate for the age group of your class.

This *Video Guide* is designed for use with the *Video Program*. The *Video Guide* provides background information and suggestions for pre-viewing, viewing, and post-viewing activities for all portions of the video program. It also contains scripts and synopses for all dramatic episodes, transcripts of all interviews and television footage, supplementary vocabulary lists, and reproducible activity masters for use with all sections of the video program.

Contents

Videocassette 1

Komm mit nach Brandenburg!
Teaching Suggestions	1
Activity Master	2

KAPITEL 1 Wer bist du?
Video Synopses	3
Teaching Suggestions	4
Activity Masters	6

KAPITEL 2 Spiel und Spaß
Video Synopses	9
Teaching Suggestions	10
Activity Masters	12

KAPITEL 3 Komm mit nach Hause!
Video Synopses	15
Teaching Suggestions	16
Activity Masters	18

Videocassette 2

Komm mit nach Schleswig-Holstein!
Teaching Suggestions	21
Activity Master	22

KAPITEL 4 Alles für die Schule!
Video Synopses	23
Teaching Suggestions	24
Activity Masters	26

KAPITEL 5 Klamotten kaufen
Video Synopses	29
Teaching Suggestions	30
Activity Masters	32

KAPITEL 6 Pläne machen
Video Synopses	35
Teaching Suggestions	36
Activity Masters	38

Videocassette 3

Komm mit nach München!
Teaching Suggestions	41
Activity Master	42

KAPITEL 7 Zu Hause helfen
Video Synopses	43
Teaching Suggestions	44
Activity Masters	46

KAPITEL 8 Einkaufen gehen
Video Synopses	49
Teaching Suggestions	50
Activity Masters	52

KAPITEL 9 Amerikaner in München
Video Synopses	55
Teaching Suggestions	56
Activity Masters	58

Videocassette 4

Komm mit nach Baden-Württemberg!
Teaching Suggestions	61
Activity Master	62

KAPITEL 10 Kino und Konzerte
Video Synopses	63
Teaching Suggestions	64
Activity Masters	66

KAPITEL 11 Der Geburtstag
Video Synopses	69
Teaching Suggestions	70
Activity Masters	72

KAPITEL 12 Die Fete
Video Synopses	75
Teaching Suggestions	76
Activity Masters	78

Video Scripts	81
Answer Key	111

Videocassette 5 contains all dramatic episodes with German captions.

Location Opener for Chapters 1-3

Location: Brandenburg

Start Time: 0:56
Length: 3:23
Student textbook pp. 12-15

The language in this location opener is authentic German spoken at a normal rate and may be difficult for students to understand. It should be made clear to them that they are not expected to understand everything. The types of activities you choose to do with them should be designed to help them understand the major points; the activities included for this section have been designed with this in mind. (script on p. 81)

Teaching Suggestions

Pre-viewing

Have students locate Brandenburg on the map on p. 2 of the textbook and identify its capital (Potsdam). Ask students to look at pp. 12-15 in the textbook and read the captions. Use the information on pp. 11A-11B of the *Teacher's Edition* for background information. Before showing the Location Opener segment of the video, ask students to watch it with the following questions in mind: Is Potsdam a large city or a small one? Is it a young city or an old one? Ask students on what they base their answers.

Viewing

Step 1 Show the video once without sound. As students are watching the Location Opener, ask them the above questions.

Step 2 Show the video again without sound, having them write down the major attractions they see in the order they see them (accept whatever level their descriptions are, including simple designations, such as *bridge* or *castle*.)

Step 3 Have students compare the attractions they saw in the video with the photos on pp. 13-15 of the textbook.

Step 4 Finally, have them work through the Supplementary Vocabulary, perhaps covering up the English first and attempting to guess at meanings. Emphasize that these words are for recognition only, to help them understand the gist of what they hear in the video.

Step 5 Have students read along as you pronounce the names of the places mentioned in Potsdam (Activity 1) and their descriptions (Activity 2). This will help students to correlate the written German with the spoken German as they complete the activities.

Step 6 Show the video with sound and have students complete the activities on p. 2. Answers to some of the more difficult questions have been included, so that students have something on which to base their guesses. You may need to show the video several times so that students can answer the questions correctly.

Post-viewing

1. Have students, in groups or in pairs, compare their answers on the Activity Master. Play the video once again, if necessary.

2. Make statements and have students say whether they are correct (**stimmt**) or incorrect (**stimmt nicht**). For example: **Die Brücke verbindet Potsdam und Frankfurt. (stimmt nicht) Potsdam ist 1000 Jahre alt. (stimmt)** Then ask questions about the sights in the video and have students look at the video for answers. Your questions might be in English, for example, "What is the name of the building where three world leaders met to sign the Potsdam agreement in 1945?" (Cecilienhof Palace)

3. Go back to the general questions about Potsdam you posed before viewing and discuss the answers. Have students defend their answers by referring to what they saw in the video.

German 1 Komm mit!   Video Guide **1**

Name _____ Klasse _____ Datum _____

 Activity Master: Location Opener

Supplementary Vocabulary			
die Hauptstadt	capital city	historisch	historic
die Brücke	bridge	die Fußgängerzone	pedestrian zone
das Chinesische Teehaus	Chinese tea house	das Schloss	castle
das Viertel	quarter	die Kirche	church
das Holländische Viertel	Dutch quarter	der Markt	marketplace
das Tor	gate	das Rathaus	city hall
die Windmühle	windmill		

Viewing

1. Jens mentions the following places to see in Potsdam. Indicate with numbers in the blanks the order in which he mentions them. Several answers are given to help you get started.

   __1__ die Glienicker Brücke   _____ die Fußgängerzone

   __2__ der Alte Markt   __7__ das Chinesische Teehaus

   __4__ das Brandenburger Tor   __9__ Schloss Cecilienhof

   _____ Babelsberger Schloss   _____ das Holländische Viertel

   _____ Schloss Sanssouci

Post-viewing

2. Match each place name on the left to an appropriate statement on the right.

   _____ 1. Potsdam   a. verbindet Berlin mit Potsdam

   __a__ 2. die Glienicker Brücke   b. das bekannteste Gebäude in Potsdam

   _____ 3. das Brandenburger Tor   c. tausend Jahre alt

   _____ 4. das Holländische Viertel   d. Rokoko Pavillon geschmückt (*decorated*) mit Musikantenfiguren

   _____ 5. Schloss Sanssouci   e. im holländischen Baustil errichtet

   _____ 6. das Chinesische Teehaus   f. wird zur Zeit renoviert

2 Video Guide   German 1 Komm mit!

KAPITEL 1 — Wer bist du?

Functions modeled in video:
- saying hello and goodbye
- asking someone's name and giving yours
- asking who someone is
- asking someone's age and giving yours
- talking about where people are from
- talking about how someone gets to school

Video Segment	Correlation to Print Materials — Pupil's Edition	Video Guide — Activity Masters	Video Guide — Scripts	Videocassette 1 — Start Time	Videocassette 1 — Length	Videocassette 5 (captioned) — Start Time	Videocassette 5 (captioned) — Length
Los geht's!	pp.18-19	p. 6	pp. 81-82	4:22	2:18	1:00	1:47
Fortsetzung		pp. 7-8	p. 82	6:42	2:09	2:49	2:05
Landeskunde	p. 31*	pp. 6, 7	pp. 82-83	9:27	2:48		
Videoclips		p. 8	p. 83	12:30	2:20		

*The *Video Program* provides film footage of the Landeskunde interviews in the *Pupil's Edition* and additional interviews.

Video Synopses

Los geht's! Vor der Schule

This segment of the video takes place on the first day of school. Several friends (Tara, Jens, and Ahmet) get to know a new student (Holger).

Fortsetzung

In the German classroom, the new teacher introduces himself and learns the names of the students. After class the students go outside to play soccer.

Landeskunde

Students from different cities in Germany tell who they are and how they get to school.

Videoclips: Werbung

1. WH Wiener Handelskammer: Chamber of commerce
2. Scout Schultaschen: school bags
3. Time Life Bücher: books

German 1 Komm mit! Video Guide 3

Teaching Suggestions

Captioned Video

Both **Los geht's!** and **Fortsetzung** are available with German captions on Videocassette 5.

Los geht's!

Pre-viewing

Ask students the following questions: How do you get to school? How do you greet your friends when you first see them at school in the morning? Do you have a specific group of friends you spend time with at school? If you were new at school, how would you go about meeting other students?

Viewing

1. As students are watching the **Los geht's!** video segment, have them listen for different ways people greet and say goodbye to each other. Have them write these expressions on a piece of paper and place a check mark beside each one every time they hear that expression used in the video.

       Hallo!   Guten Morgen!   Morgen!   Tschüs!

   Have them tell you which of the above expressions are saying hello and which are saying goodbye.

2. For further practice with the expressions in the **Los geht's!** segment, see Activity Master 1, p. 6.

Post-viewing

3. After students have viewed the **Los geht's!** segment at least once, have them open their books and follow along as you play the video again. Have them identify and tell you who uses each of the greetings and farewells listed in number 1 above.

4. Ask students if the way the teenagers in the videos introduce themselves to each other is similar to or different from the way they would introduce each other. Have students guess on what kind of team Ahmet is **die Nummer Eins**.

Fortsetzung

Pre-viewing

Ask students: How do you normally address your teachers? How do you think German students might address theirs? Do you think a German classroom might be more or less formal than an American one? What do you think most German students' favorite sport is? Do you participate in sports? Which ones? What do you do together with your friends?

Viewing

See **Viewing** activity on Activity Master 2, p. 7.

Post-viewing

Have students decide whether their idea about the formality of German classrooms (See **Pre-viewing** activity above) was accurate or not. Ask them how they might have come up with the opinion they had before viewing the video.

Landeskunde

Pre-viewing
Take a survey in your class to determine how students get to school. Expand the survey with information from students about how their friends and/or siblings get to school. Ask students if people who live in different areas (cities, suburbs, farms, for example) might get to school in different ways. Have students brainstorm German vocabulary for ways of getting to school (means of transportation).

Viewing
Before viewing the **Landeskunde** segment, have students write the names of the teenagers who are interviewed. You will have to give your students a list of the names, since they do not all appear in the *Pupil's Edition*. As students watch the video and listen to the interviews, have them write beside each name how that person gets to school.

Post-viewing
Compare the results of the students' in-class survey with the interviewed students in the **Landeskunde** segment. Have students tell you (or each other in pairs or small groups) what similarities or differences there are between the responses of German and American students.

Have students find on the map the cities of the students interviewed. Have them hypothesize whether Bietigheim, Hamburg, and Berlin might be larger or smaller cities, based on the students' answers to the interview question.

Videoclips: Werbung

Pre-viewing
Have students look at the first three questions of the **Viewing** activities on p. 8 to familiarize themselves with the possible answers.

Viewing
First play the commercials without sound and see if students are able to answer the first three questions on p. 8 (1., 2., and 3. of number 8). Now play the commercials with sound. Have students confirm their answers to the first three questions. Play the commercials again and have them answer the last three questions on the Activity Master.

Post-viewing
1. Have students listen to the **WHK** ad again and compare the alphabet they hear with the alphabet they learned in the **Vorschau**. See if they can identify the two letters that are pronounced differently in the video (J is pronounced "yea" on the video and Q is pronounced "kvay.") Explain to them that such pronunciation differences generally have to do with regional variations. Since this is an ad for the **Wiener Handelskammer (WHK)**, can students guess in what German-speaking area this pronunciation of the letters **j** and **q** is standard? (Austria)

2. In order to tie the second commercial back to the **Los geht's!** segment, ask in German: **Wer von Holgers neuen Freunden ist die Nummer Eins im Team?** (Ahmet)

3. Have students locate Mecklenburg-Vorpommern on the map on p. 2 of their textbooks. Have them identify the **Bundesländer** shown on the other books in the commercial. Have them find those **Bundesländer** on the map.

Name _____ Klasse _____ Datum _____

Activity Master 1

Los geht's!

Viewing

1. Listen to the video and identify the words from the box that go in each blank to complete what Jens, Tara, Holger, and Ahmet say to each other.

   1. Ist das dein Moped?
      Ja. _____ ! _____ !

   Box: aus Klasse! neu heißt Ja, klar! Super!

   2. Hallo! Wer bist du denn?
      Bist du _____ hier?

   3. Morgen, Holger! Woher kommst du denn?
      _____ Walburg.

   4. Sag mal, Ahmet. Ist morgen Training?
      _____ ! Um 3 Uhr.

   5. Ich bin Holger. Wie _____ du? — Ahmet. Ahmet Özkan.

2. Say whether the following statements are true (**stimmt**) or false (**stimmt nicht**). Correct the false statements by supplying the correct person's name for each statement.

stimmt	stimmt nicht		
_____	_____	1.	Jens (_____) kommt mit dem Moped zur Schule.
_____	_____	2.	Ahmet (_____) kommt aus Walburg.
_____	_____	3.	Tara (_____) ist neu hier.
_____	_____	4.	Holger (_____) kommt aus der Türkei.
_____	_____	5.	Ahmet (_____) ist die Nummer Eins im Team.

Landeskunde (in *Pupil's Edition*)

Viewing

3. Draw a line matching the person with the way he or she gets to school. Note that some students use more than one way to get to school. Draw a line to all the modes of transportation they mention.

Christina

Sonja

Sandra

Johannes

Tim

U

Name _____ Klasse _____ Datum _____

 Activity Master 2

Landeskunde (on Video only)

Supplementary Vocabulary
das Leichtkraftrad=Moped
selten *seldom*   die Viertelstunde *quarter-hour*

KAPITEL 1

Viewing

1. Place a mark next to each mode of transportation as it is mentioned. When you have finished, add up the marks to find out how many students use each mode of transportation.

   _____ mit dem    _____ zu

   _____ mit dem    _____ mit dem

   _____ mit dem    _____ mit der

Post-viewing

2. All of the Bietigheim students who were interviewed get to school by bus, by bike, or on foot. Bietigheim is a city near Stuttgart. Find Stuttgart on the map on p. 2 of your textbook. Do you think Bietigheim has a subway system? Why or why not?

   _____
   _____

Fortsetzung

Supplementary Vocabulary

Ruhe, bitte!	*Quiet, please!*	dein Nachname	*your last name*
euer	*your* (pl)	eine kleine Stadt	*small town*
Fangen wir … an!	*Let's get started!*	am Schwarzen Meer	*on the Black Sea*

Viewing

3. Wie heißt der Lehrer?   Herr Lohmann   Herr Gärtner   Herr Özkan

4. Circle the names of the students who introduce themselves in the class.
   Claudia   Norbert   Harald   Ulla   Jens   Karsten   Handan   Holger
   Birgit   Beate   Ahmet   Max   Steffi Tara   Ursula   Anja

5. Wie sagt man „tschüs" auf türkisch?   hej da   jo napot   Güle Güle

Post-viewing

6. In groups of five or six, re-enact the first day of class. One student is the teacher, the others are the students. The teacher introduces himself or herself to the others and says where he or she is from, then asks the others their names. List the phrases you will need in order to play these roles.

   _____
   _____

German 1 Komm mit!   Video Guide **7**
Copyright © by Holt, Rinehart and Winston. All rights reserved.

Name _____ Klasse _____ Datum _____

 Activity Master 3

7. Do you know any students who were born in other countries? Who are they and where do they come from? Make a list here. Try to find out how to say the names of the countries in German.

   _____
   _____
   _____
   _____

Videoclips: Werbung

Viewing

8. What do you think each commercial is advertising?

   | **Supplementary Vocabulary** |
   | die deutschen Länder *the German states* |

   1. **Werbung 1**
      a. a bank   b. the German post office   c. a phonics reading program
   2. **Werbung 2**
      a. snack crackers b. camping equipment   c. school bags
   3. **Werbung 3**
      a. books about fishing
      b. books about the German states
      c. books about popular German personalities

9. What is the name of the company advertised in **Werbung 1**?
   a. HKW   b. KWH   c. WHK

10. According to the boy in **Werbung 2**, what are **Scout Schultaschen**?
    a. Spitze!   b. die Nummer Eins!   c. Prima!

11. In **Werbung 3**, which **Bundesland** is the first book about?
    a. Brandenburg   b. Baden-Württemberg   c. Mecklenburg-Vorpommern

Post-viewing

12. Get together in pairs or groups and discuss the following questions. One person will act as secretary and write the answers. Be prepared to report your findings to the class.
    a. In which ad was the product easiest to identify? Why? What clues made the products easy or difficult to identify?
    b. If the possible answers to question number **8.1.** were **a.** a bank, **b.** a brokerage firm, or **c.** a mortgage company, would you have been able to guess the correct answer? Why or why not? Would a German have been able to guess the right answer? Why or why not?
    c. Rate each ad according to its similarity to or difference from ads you see in this country. A rating of 1 is very different, and 5 is similar. What do your ratings tell you about German television advertising?
    d. Name as many non-language clues as you can think of that helped you identify the products. Are there more clues here than you listed in **12.a.** above? Make a list that includes all the clues you have thought of.

8 Video Guide   German 1 Komm mit!

Copyright © by Holt, Rinehart and Winston. All rights reserved.

KAPITEL 2 — Spiel und Spaß

Functions modeled in video:
- talking about interests
- expressing likes and dislikes
- saying when you do various activities
- asking for an opinion and expressing yours
- agreeing and disagreeing

Video Segment	Correlation to Print Materials			Videocassette 1		Videocassette 5 (captioned)	
	Pupil's Edition	*Video Guide* Activity Masters	Scripts	Start Time	Length	Start Time	Length
Los geht's!	pp. 44-45	p. 12	p. 83	15:05	2:13	5:00	2:15
Fortsetzung		pp. 13-14	pp. 83-84	17:20	2:06	7:16	2:06
Landeskunde	p. 54*	pp. 12, 13	pp. 84-85	20:06	3:44		
Videoclips		p. 14	p. 85	25:05	2:35		

*The *Video Program* provides film footage of the Landeskunde interviews in the *Pupil's Edition* and additional interviews.

 Video Synopses

Los geht's! *Was machst du in deiner Freizeit?*

In this segment of the video, Holger finds his new friends Tara, Jens, and Ahmet playing a card game in the school yard. They ask Holger about his hobbies and interests and discover they share many, but not all, of the same interests.

Fortsetzung

Holger finds out how much tennis lessons cost, and then does odd jobs (mowing the lawn, babysitting, washing the car, etc.) to earn the money for lessons. He works hard at learning tennis, and the next time Tara and Steffi are going to play tennis, he joins them. Tara is impressed that he has learned so much so fast.

Landeskunde

Students of various ages talk about what they like to do in their free time.

Videoclips: Werbung

1. **Nesfit:** sports drink
2. **Isostar:** sports drink
3. **Cebion Plus Magnesium:** magnesium tablets
4. **Wasserpark Alpamare:** water park
5. **Fremdenverkehrsverein Tirol:** tourism

German 1 Komm mit!

Teaching Suggestions

Captioned Video
Both **Los geht's!** and **Fortsetzung** are available with German captions on Videocassette 5.

Los geht's!

Pre-viewing
Have students brainstorm German vocabulary for **Freizeitaktivitäten**. Ask them which activities they like to do. Ask them if they think German students have different hobbies. Why do they think that?

Viewing
See **Viewing** activities on Activity Master 1, p. 12.

Post-viewing
Ask students why they think Holger is upset at the end of the episode. See how many people in the class have the same hobbies as Holger. How many do and do not play tennis? Cards? Have students make a list on the board of the activities mentioned and have them say whether Holger likes them or not, then whether they (your students) like them or not.

Fortsetzung

Pre-viewing
Why do students think Holger might not like tennis? Have students suggest what they might do next in Holger's position. How much do they think tennis lessons might cost, and where could they get the money for them if they did not have it?

Viewing
See **Viewing** activities on Activity Master 2, p. 13.

Post-viewing
1. Ask questions in English to make sure students understood what Holger did and why. In the video segment, what do tennis lessons cost for students? For non-students? What did Tara think about Holger's skills as a tennis player?

2. Make sure students understood the video segment by making **stimmt/stimmt nicht** statements. After students tell you whether your statements are true or false, have them correct any false statements. For example, **Ahmet, Tara und Jens spielen Tennis.** (stimmt nicht: Sie spielen Karten.) **Holger spielt Karten sehr gern.** (stimmt nicht: Holger spielt Karten nicht so gern.)

3. Write on pieces of paper sentences that retell the **Fortsetzung**. Have students work in pairs and listen to the video again, then put the sentences in order. When all the groups have finished, read the sentences from one group aloud. The rest of the students should listen carefully and make any corrections. (Note: Having students do this in German will be difficult for them now, but it will help them begin to prepare for grammar and vocabulary that they will learn later: word order, days of the week, and names of chores.) Some suggested sentences to use for this activity:

Am Montag schlägt (*hits*) er den Ball gar nicht.
Am Dienstag schlägt er den Ball zu hart — der Ball geht zu weit.
Am Mittwoch spielt er besser.
Am Donnerstag spielt er gut.
Am Freitag spielt er super — wie Boris Becker!
Tara sagt, sie und Steffi spielen Tennis.
Holger spielt mit.
Tara sagt, Holger spielt prima und lernt schnell.

Landeskunde

Pre-viewing

Have students brainstorm German vocabulary for **Freizeitaktivitäten**. (Supply extra vocabulary as necessary.) Take a class survey. For each activity named, find out how many like to do it and how many do not. Have students write down the activities on a piece of paper for use during viewing.

Viewing

Have students put a mark next to the activities on their papers as they hear the German students say they like to do them. Have them try to write down the activities they hear that are not on their list (even if they get only some sort of phonetic approximation).

Post-viewing

Have students compare the list they made from the video with the list they made in their class survey. What differences did they find between the interests of German and American teenagers? Help them with any activities they heard but were not sure how to spell.

Videoclips: Werbung

Show ads twice. The first time, have students say in English what the ads are for. The second time, have them write down in German the activities they see. For the **Wasserbahnpark** and the Tirol ads, ask **Was kann man in einem Wasserbahnpark tun? Was kann man in den Alpen tun?**

Name _____ Klasse _____ Datum _____

 Activity Master 1

Los geht's!

Supplementary Vocabulary			
Mau-Mau	a popular card game	gewinnen	to win
mogeln	to cheat	verlieren	to lose
Ski laufen	to ski	Lieblingssport	favorite sport

Viewing

1. Circle the activities that Holger says he likes to do.

Ski laufen	tanzen	Tennis spielen	Musik hören
Gitarre spielen	singen	Briefmarken sammeln	Fußball spielen
Karten spielen	Golf spielen	schwimmen	wandern

2. Circle the activities that Holger says he does not like to do.

Ski laufen	tanzen	Tennis spielen	Musik hören
Gitarre spielen	singen	Briefmarken sammeln	Fußball spielen
Karten spielen	Golf spielen	schwimmen	wandern

Post-viewing

3. In the list of activities in number 1 above, underline the activities you like to do.

4. In the list of activities in number 2, underline the activities that you do not like to do.

5. List any interests that you and Holger have in common.
   _____

6. List any dislikes that you and Holger have in common.

7. Interview several students to find at least two who have interests in common with Holger. Write their names and the common interest(s).
   _____

Landeskunde (in *Pupil's Edition*)

Viewing

8. Match the people with their interests.

   _____ 1. Michael
   _____ 2. Christina
   _____ 3. Elke
   _____ 4. Björn
   _____ 5. Heide

   a.   b.   c.   d.   e.

Post-viewing

9. a. Which interviewee has interests most like your own? _____

   b. What are those interests? _____

KAPITEL 2

12 Video Guide

German 1 Komm mit!

Copyright © by Holt, Rinehart and Winston. All rights reserved.

Name _____ Klasse _____ Datum _____

Activity Master 2

Landeskunde (on Video only)

Supplementary Vocabulary			
mutig	*courageous*	die Geduld	*patience*
höher	*higher*	die Bälle	*(tennis) balls*

Pre-viewing

1. Make a list in German of as many free-time activities as you can think of.
   _____
   _____

Viewing

2. Circle any activities you hear that are on your list above. In the space below, write down activities you hear that are not on your list. If you aren't sure how to spell these activities correctly, write an approximation.
   _____
   _____

Post-viewing

3. Get together in groups of three or four and compare your lists from the **Pre-viewing** activities. Are there activities on your list that not everybody in the group knows? Try to explain what they are by acting them out. Go around in the group until everybody understands all the activities on everybody's lists.

4. Compare the activities you wrote down during the video with those of the other people in your group. Together try to figure out what each word you heard but didn't quite understand means. Look these words up in the dictionary if no one in the group can figure them out.

Fortsetzung

Supplementary Vocabulary			
die Geduld	*patience*	die Bälle höher nehmen	
ruhiger	*calmer*		*to pick off the balls higher*
mutiger	*more daring(ly)*		

Viewing

5. What advice does the instructor give Holger?

   a. _____ mehr Geduld haben   d. _____ auf den Ball konzentrieren

   b. _____ mit Tara und Steffi spielen   e. _____ mit Boris Becker spielen

   c. _____ ruhiger spielen   f. _____ mutiger spielen

KAPITEL 2

German 1 Komm mit! Video Guide **13**
Copyright © by Holt, Rinehart and Winston. All rights reserved.

Name _____ Klasse _____ Datum _____

 Activity Master 3

6. To which tennis player does Holger's teacher compare Holger?
   Björn Borg   Steffi Graf   Boris Becker

Post-viewing

7. Why did Holger regret saying that he didn't like tennis?
   _____

8. Why do you think Holger now says he likes tennis?
   _____

Videoclips: Werbung

Supplementary Vocabulary			
beschlossen	*decided*	veränderte sich alles	*everything changed*
zusammen	*together*	scheint	*seems*
Mut machen	*to encourage*	(die) Stärke	*strength*
wieder aufbauen	*build up again*	..., darauf kommt es an!	*That's the main thing!*
fehlen	*to be missing*		

Pre-viewing

9. What activities do you like to do that are really strenuous? Write them (in German) in the blank.
   _____

Viewing

10. Draw a line matching the products advertised in the first three commercials with the activity depicted in the ad.

    Nesfit

    Isostar

    Cebion Plus Magnesium

11. Was kann man im Wasserbahnpark Alpamare tun? Underline the activities you see.
    schwimmen   relaxen   Klavier spielen
    Fahrrad fahren   Golf spielen   Schach spielen
    basteln   Fußball spielen im Wasser spielen

Post-viewing

12. List the things you recall seeing people do in Tirol. _____
    _____

13. With a partner or in small groups, compare your lists and prepare a longer list of activities available in Tirol. Use a dictionary to look up words you don't know in German. Share your completed list with the class.

KAPITEL 3  Komm mit nach Hause!

Functions modeled in video:
- talking about where you and others live
- offering something to eat and drink, and responding to an offer
- saying please, thank you, and you're welcome
- describing a room
- talking about family members
- describing people

Video Segment	Correlation to Print Materials			Videocassette 1		Videocassette 5 (captioned)	
	Pupil's Edition	Video Guide		Start Time	Length	Start Time	Length
		Activity Masters	Scripts				
Los geht's!	pp. 70–71	p. 18	pp. 85-86	27:00	3:28	9:28	3:31
Fortsetzung		pp. 19–20	p. 86	30:30	1:37	13:01	1:36
Landeskunde	p. 77*	pp. 18, 19	p. 86	32:45	1:37		
Videoclips		p. 20	p. 86-87	34:36	3:54		

* The *Video Program* provides film footage of the Landeskunde interviews in the *Pupil's Edition* and additional interviews.

Video Synopses

Los geht's! *Bei Jens zu Hause!*
In this segment of the video, Jens invites Holger to his house after school. The boys have a snack, and Jens shows Holger his room. Later Jens' cousin comes to visit, and Holger is surprised to find that Jens' cousin is Tara.

Fortsetzung
Tara, Jens, and Holger go to Ahmet's house, where Tara is going to tutor Ahmet's cousin, Handan. As Tara and Handan go inside to study, Jens, Ahmet, and Holger go to play soccer.

Landeskunde
People from different cities talk about where they live.

Videoclips: Werbung
1. **Apfel Botschaft Bodensee:** apples
2. **Spezi:** soda
3. **Apollinaris Mineralwasser:** mineral water
4. **Pom-Bär:** chips
5. **Gold Fischli:** crackers
6. **BHW:** bank

German 1 Komm mit! — Video Guide

Teaching Suggestions

Captioned Video
Both **Los geht's!** and **Fortsetzung** are available with German captions on Videocassette 5.

Los geht's!

Pre-viewing
Have students describe a typical afternoon after school. Ask them questions about their routine: How do they get home? Do they go with a friend? When do they do their homework? Do they have afternoon snacks? Have them name some of the things they eat and drink after school.

Viewing
See **Viewing** activity on Activity Master 1, p. 18.

Post-viewing
1. Have students tell you about Jens' family: his mother's name, the names and ages of siblings, his cousin's name and age.
2. Ask students what posters they have on their walls. Ask them if they can guess who Patricia Kaas is, or what she does. Tell them that she is a famous French singer who sings in several languages.
3. Ask students why Holger is so surprised to find out that Tara is Jens' cousin.

Fortsetzung

Pre-viewing
Ask students if they do their homework alone or with friends. Ask them if they've ever tutored someone or were tutored by someone. In what subjects?

Viewing
See **Viewing** activity on Activity Master 2, p. 19.

Post-viewing
1. See if students can tell you what Tara and Handan look like. Have them describe the girls in German if they can. Ask if there are any girls in the class who fit the same description.
2. See if students can tell you in what subject Tara is especially strong. In what subject is she tutoring Handan?

Landeskunde

Pre-viewing
1. Have students do a survey to find out where everyone in the class lives (in what neighborhood, if in a city; in which suburb, etc.). Ask students if they know students who live in the city; in the country; in a suburb. If so, how do those students get to school?
2. Have students write their addresses (without their names) on slips of paper; collect these for later use.

Viewing
See **Viewing** activities on Activity Masters 1 and 2, pp. 18 and 19.

Post-viewing
1. Have your students work in pairs and listen to the video segment again, and then try to match the students' names with where they live. When they have done that, have them switch groups and ask and answer questions with their new partner about where each student lives. For example, **Wo wohnt Thorsten Weyrauch? Er wohnt in Eichwald.**

2. Randomly hand out the slips of paper with students' addresses. Have students ask other students their addresses in order to find the person whose address is on the slip of paper they have. They should ask **Wo wohnst du?** or **Wohnst du in der ____straße?**

Videoclips: Werbung

Pre-viewing

Have students list their favorite snacks and drinks, then have them brainstorm German vocabulary they have learned for snacks and drinks.

Viewing

Have students keep track of how many ads are for things to eat and how many are for things to drink. For the **BHW** commercial (the last one), have them figure out in what specific way this financial institution can be of help. (building a house; provides starting up money and long range financing for building)

Post-viewing

Have students play the role of being at someone's house after school and offering, asking for, and accepting the snacks and drinks advertised in the commercials they just saw.

Name _____ Klasse _____ Datum _____

 Activity Master 1

Los geht's!

Viewing

1. Circle the correct answer.
   1. Wie kommt Holger mit Jens nach Hause?
      mit dem Bus   mit dem Auto   mit dem Fahrrad   mit dem Moped
   2. Was möchte Holger trinken?
      eine Limo   eine Cola   Mineralwasser   Tee
   3. Was essen Jens und Holger?
      ein Stück Obst   ein Stück Kuchen   ein paar Kekse

Post-viewing

2. Answer the questions.
   1. Wie heißt Jens' Kusine? _____
   2. Why is Holger so surprised to find out who Jens' cousin is?
      _____
      _____
   3. Why does Jens tell Holger **Mensch, du denkst zu viel**?
      _____
      _____

Landeskunde (in *Pupil's Edition*)

Viewing

3. In the blanks under each student's name, write the name of the city, school, or address you hear each student mention.

   Hamburg   Pinneberg   Türkei   Gustav-Falke-Straße
   München   Reichenau-Schule   Italien

Dominick	Jasmin	Johanna	Thomas	Ingo
_____	_____	_____	_____	____
_____	_____	_____	_____	____
_____	_____	_____	_____	____
_____	_____	_____	_____	____

KAPITEL 3

18 Video Guide   German 1 Komm mit!

Name _____ Klasse _____ Datum _____

Activity Master 2

Landeskunde (on Video only)

Viewing

1. When these people were asked where they live, some said the name of their city, some said the name of a city near their home, some said which part of the city they live in, and some said what city they come from. How many people said each thing? Keep a tally.

   _____ city name   _____ part of the city

   _____ which city they are near   _____ the city they are from

Post-viewing

2. In groups or with a partner, compare your answers. If there are discrepancies in your numbers, check your results by asking each other **Wo wohnt ...?** and going over all the students' responses. Now ask your partner (or, if in a group, your partners) **Wo wohnst du? Woher kommst du?** Record the answers you get.

   _____
   _____
   _____
   _____

Fortsetzung

Supplementary Vocabulary
Wohin gehst du? — Where are you going?   das Genie — *genius*
mit den Hausaufgaben helfen — *to help with homework*   Lernt fleißig! — *Study hard!*
Was für Fächer ...? — *Which subjects...?*

Viewing

3. Circle the correct answer.

   1. In which subjects does Tara help Ahmet's cousin?
      Geschichte   Erdkunde   Mathe   Deutsch   Englisch

   2. Wie sieht Ahmets Kusine aus?
      blonde Haare, blaue Augen   rotbraune Haare, dunkle Augen
      blonde Haare, dunkle Augen   schwarze Haare, blaue Augen

   3. Wie heißt Ahmets Kusine?
      Anna   Handan   Liselotte   Amir   Marjam

KAPITEL 3

Name _____ Klasse _____ Datum _____

Activity Master 3

Post-viewing

4. Answer the questions.

   1. Wie sieht deine Traumfreundin (dein Traumfreund) aus?

      _____
      _____
      _____

   2. Jens says **Tara ist ein Genie in Mathe.** Are you, or would you like to be a **Genie** in a particular subject? If so, in which one?

      _____
      _____
      _____

Videoclips: Werbung

Supplementary Vocabulary			
achten	*to pay attention to*	bewundern	*to admire*
unvergleichlich	*incomparable*	knusprig	*crisp*
verführerisch	*tempting*	knabbern	*to nibble, munch*

Viewing

5. Match the brand name with the product.

   _____ 1. Apfel Botschaft Bodensee   a. etwas zum Knabbern
   _____ 2. Spezi   b. Mineralwasser
   _____ 3. Apollinaris   c. Cola-Limo
   _____ 4. Pom-Bär   d. Startgeld zum Bauen
   _____ 5. Gold Fischli   e. Obst
   _____ 6. BHW   f. Kartoffelsnack

Post-viewing

6. Match each of the ads you have seen with the appropriate statement that describes what happens in the ad.

   _____ 1. the ad in which Oliver's friend admires his **Lebensstil**   a. Goldfischli
   _____ 2. the ad that talks about **der erste Wolf, der backen kann**   b. Pom-Bär
   _____ 3. the ad that features a **spezielle Knabbertechnik,**   c. BHW
            which is described as **eine starke Nummer**   d. Spezi
   _____ 4. the ad that offers **Ideen für mehr Lebensqualität**

Location Opener for Chapters 4-6

Location: Schleswig-Holstein

Start Time: 1:17
Length: 3:27
Student textbook pp. 96-99

The language in this location opener is authentic German spoken at a normal rate and may be difficult for students to understand. It should be made clear to them that they are not expected to understand everything. The types of activities you choose to do with them should be designed to help them understand the major points; the activities included for this section have been designed with this in mind. (script on p. 87)

Teaching Suggestions

Pre-viewing

1. Have students locate the state of Schleswig-Holstein on the map on p. 2 of their textbooks. Tell them that Wedel lies down-river from Hamburg, and have them locate Hamburg and the river that runs through it. Have them identify the river. (Elbe)

2. Go through pp. 98-99 in the *Pupil's Edition* with the students. Use the information in the *Teacher's Edition* on pp. 95A-95B to provide background information about Schleswig-Holstein in general.

3. Before showing the Location Opener, ask students to watch it with the following questions in mind: What clues in the photos tell them about the general location of Schleswig-Holstein and Wedel in particular? Do they think Wedel is a young, modern city or an older, traditional city? On what do they base their opinion?

Viewing

Step 1 Show the video once without sound and discuss with the class the answers to the above questions about Wedel. They may not have enough information to answer them yet, but they will get more information each time they view the segment.

Step 2 Show the video again without sound, having them write down the major attractions they see in the order they see them. (Let them use simple answers, such as *shipping* or *marketplace*, as long as they accurately convey what is in the photo.)

Step 3 Help students work their way through the Supplementary Vocabulary on p. 22. Help students see that they can make intelligent guesses about meaning by looking for cognates.

Step 4 Show the video with sound, and have students complete the Location Opener activities on p. 22.

Post-viewing

1. Have students, working either in pairs or groups, compare their answers on the Activity Master. Play the video once again if necessary.

2. Make statements and have students say whether they are correct (**stimmt**) or incorrect (**stimmt nicht**), eg: **Wedel liegt an der Oder** or **Wedel ist in der Nähe von Stuttgart**. Have them correct the statements which are false. Play the video again and repeat the true/false statements. Or make a statement, then play the corresponding part of the video and have students answer **stimmt/stimmt nicht**. Continue in this way until you are confident that students understand the material.

3. Go back to the general questions about Wedel you posed before viewing and discuss the answers. Have students defend their answers by referring to what they saw in the video. Lead students in a discussion of some cultural issues by asking the following question:

   Is Wedel important historically? Have them tell you why or why not.

German 1 Komm mit! Video Guide **21**

Name _____ Klasse _____ Datum _____

Activity Master: Location Opener

Supplementary Vocabulary

das Schiff	ship	das historische Viertel	historic quarter
der Markt	market	der Bildhauer	sculptor
die Wassermühle	water mill	der Teich	pond
der Hafen	harbor	das Boot	boat
das Freibad	open-air pool	das Ausflugsziel	excursion goal/ destination
das Wahrzeichen	landmark		

Viewing

1. As you watch the Location Opener segment, circle the correct answer or answers to these questions.

   1. Wedel liegt an welchem Fluss?
      Weser   Oder   Elbe   Neckar   Rhein

   2. Wann findet der Wochenmarkt am Marktplatz im historischen Viertel statt?
      Mittwoch u. Freitag   Montag u. Mittwoch   Dienstag u. Freitag

   3. Was sind die Wahrzeichen Wedels?
      Schloss Sanssouci   der Anker   das Hexenwegle
      der Viktualienmarkt   das Münchner Kindl   der Roland
      das Reepschläger Haus   das Brandenburger Tor

   4. Wann ist das Freibad geöffnet?
      jeden Tag   von März bis Dezember   von 7.30 bis 21.00   Mai bis September

2. Complete these phrases by matching the numbered partial phrases with the appropriate endings.

   1. Das historische Zentrum Wedels   a. ist heute ein Museum.
   2. Das Geburtshaus von Ernst Barlach   b. ist ein Theaterschiff.
   3. Hier ist die Wassermühle   c. liegt am Marktplatz.
   4. So eine Dampferfahrt   d. macht natürlich schon viel Spaß.
   5. Die „Batavia"   e. mit dem Mühlenteich.

Post-viewing

3. Circle all the answers that apply to the following questions, then discuss the answers with a partner or in groups.

   1. Wedel is
      a. a small city   b. an old city   c. a young city   d. a large city

   2. People from Hamburg probably travel to Wedel to
      a. go shopping   c. go swimming   e. go to the opera or theater
      b. go sailing   d. enjoy the outdoors

4. Can you think of a city in your country that may be very similar to Wedel in size and industry? Write two sentences describing it.

   _____
   _____
   _____

22 Video Guide   German 1 Komm mit!

KAPITEL 4 — Alles für die Schule!

Functions modeled in video:
- talking about class schedules
- using a schedule to talk about time
- sequencing events
- expressing likes, dislikes, and favorites
- responding to good news and bad news
- talking about prices
- pointing things out

Video Segment	Correlation to Print Materials			Videocassette 2		Videocassette 5 (captioned)	
	Pupil's Edition	*Video Guide* Activity Masters	*Video Guide* Scripts	Start Time	Length	Start Time	Length
Los geht's!	pp. 102–103	p. 26	pp. 87-88	4:47	4:37	14:44	4:36
Fortsetzung		pp. 27–28	p. 88	9:24	2:46	19:22	2:46
Landeskunde	p. 113*	pp. 26, 27	pp. 88-90	12:49	6:17		
Videoclips		p. 28	p. 90	19:22	1:32		

*The *Video Program* provides film footage of the Landeskunde interviews in the *Pupil's Edition* and additional interviews.

 ## Video Synopses

Los geht's! *Lars kauft Schulsachen*

In this segment of the video, a group of friends (Lars, Julia, Sina, and Alex) are at school talking about their class schedules and grades. Later, Julia runs into Lars at a stationery shop where they look at school supplies. Lars drops all of his things and discovers that his calculator does not work.

Fortsetzung

Lars and Julia return to the stationery shop to find out what is wrong with Lars' new calculator. It turns out that he just needs batteries, which he buys. They meet Sina, who is here to buy various items.

Landeskunde

Students from different cities talk about the school subjects they like, do well in, and don't like.

Videoclips: Werbung

1. Herlitz Mickey Mouse Schultaschen: school bags
2. Joker System Schultaschen: school bags
3. Läufer Schreibunterlagen: writing pads
4. Läufer Papierkörbe: wastebaskets

German 1 Komm mit!   Video Guide **23**

Teaching Suggestions

Captioned Video
Both **Los geht's!** and **Fortsetzung** are available with German captions on Videocassette 5.

Los geht's!

Pre-viewing
1. Explain that German students have their classes at different times on different days, but that their entire class (9B, for example) will have the same schedule. Ask students how this differs from American students' schedules. Have pairs of students quiz each other about their schedules, when certain subjects meet, who likes which subjects, and who dislikes which subjects.
2. Have the students outline some steps that could be taken by a student having difficulties with a class to improve his or her performance. Ask students which things one could buy at a school supplies store to help one do a better job in such subjects as math, German, English, history, or physics, etc.

Viewing
See **Viewing** activity on Activity Master 1, p. 26.

Post-viewing
Ask students if they use a calculator in their math classes. Do a survey among the people in the class who own calculators: Do the calculators have different prices? Does Lars' cost more or less than the average calculator in your class?

Fortsetzung

Pre-viewing
Ask students what they think Lars 1) should do 2) will do in this situation.

Viewing
See **Viewing** activity on Activity Master 2, p. 27.

Post-viewing
Have students discuss money. Would they have lent Lars the money as generously as Julia did? Would they have been able to get the money to pay Julia back from their parent or guardian? Have them discuss whether they think Lars and his money situation reflects something inherent in German culture, and, if so, whether it's different from North American culture.

Landeskunde

Pre-viewing
Have students list their favorite and least favorite subjects. Have them do a quick class survey to see which is the most and the least popular subject among the students in the class.

Viewing
Give your students the names of all the students interviewed and have them write beside each name the favorite and least-liked subjects. Then make a chart that shows all the answers together.

Post-viewing
Have students compare the lists made in the **Pre-viewing** activity above with the survey of interviewees. What statements can they make comparing the courses that American students and German students like and dislike?

Videoclips: Werbung

Pre-viewing
Ask students to list school supplies that they generally have to buy and tell where they buy them. Make a class survey.

Viewing
See **Viewing** activity on Activity Master 2, p. 28.

Post-viewing
Have students compare these ads to American ads for the same products. Have them design an ad for another **Schultasche**, or for another school supply product.

Name _____ Klasse _____ Datum _____

 Activity Master 1

Los geht's!

Supplementary Vocabulary			
die Mathearbeit	math test	geben	to give
So ein Mist!	Darn! Rats! What a bummer!	das ganze Zeug	all my stuff
So ein Pech!	Darn! Rats! What a bummer!	kaputt	broken
die Brille	eyeglasses		

Viewing

1. Fill in the blanks with the correct answers.

    1. Was hat Lars in Mathe?   eine _____
    2. Wie viel kostet der Taschenrechner?   _____ Euro
    3. Wie viel Geld hat Lars dabei?   _____ Euro
    4. Wer gibt Lars das Geld?   _____
    5. Was ist kaputt? _____

Post-viewing

2. Write in the blank the name of the person who might have made the following statements: **Julia, Lars,** or the **Verkäuferin.**

    _____ 1. In Mathe hab ich immer schlechte Noten.
    _____ 2. Ich habe Mathe gern. Das ist mein Lieblingsfach.
    _____ 3. Der Rechner kostet sechzehn Euro.
    _____ 4. Ich habe nur zehn Euro dabei.
    _____ 5. Ich gebe dir das Geld.
    _____ 6. So ein Pech! Der Rechner ist kaputt!

Landeskunde (in *Pupil's Edition*)

Supplementary Vocabulary			
Leistungskurs	major area of study	Gemeinschaftskunde	sociology
unsere Vorfahren	our ancestors	BK=Bildende Kunst	painting, drawing
darstellendes Spielen	theater (extracurricular)		

Viewing

3. For the following students, circle the subjects they say they like and cross out the subjects they say they don't like. (Hint: not everybody names subjects they don't like.)

Jasmin	Arbeitslehre	Mathe	Physik	Sport	Englisch
Michael	Mathe	Physik	Kunst	Chemie	Mathe
Dirk	Englisch	Spanisch	Französisch	Musik	Physik
Lugana	Englisch	Deutsch	Chemie	Spanisch	Latein
Björn	Physik	Mathematik	Informatik	Englisch	Kunst

26 Video Guide   German 1 Komm mit!

Name _____ Klasse _____ Datum _____

 Activity Master 2

Landeskunde (on Video only)

Pre-viewing

1. Ask five people in the class: **Was ist dein Lieblingsfach? Welches Fach magst du nicht so gern?** Record their answers here:

Name	Lieblingsfach	kein Lieblingsfach
1. _____	_____	_____
2. _____	_____	_____
3. _____	_____	_____
4. _____	_____	_____
5. _____	_____	_____

Viewing

2. In the group marked **Lieblingsfächer** below, put a tally mark next to each **Fach** the students interviewed in the video say they like. Put a tally mark in the second group next to each subject the students say they don't like.

Lieblingsfächer		Fächer, die sie nicht so gern haben	
_____ Arbeitslehre	_____ Informatik	_____ Arbeitslehre	_____ Informatik
_____ Biologie	_____ Kunst	_____ Biologie	_____ Kunst
_____ Chemie	_____ Mathe	_____ Chemie	_____ Mathe
_____ Deutsch	_____ Musik	_____ Deutsch	_____ Musik
_____ Englisch	_____ Physik	_____ Englisch	_____ Physik
_____ Erdkunde	_____ Religion	_____ Erdkunde	_____ Religion
_____ Französisch	_____ Spanisch	_____ Französisch	_____ Spanisch
_____ Geschichte	_____ Sport	_____ Geschichte	_____ Sport

Post-viewing

3. 1. In groups of three or four, compare your answers to the **Viewing** exercise. If necessary, ask your teacher to show the **Landeskunde** part of the video again, to see if you can all agree on the numbers of responses.
   2. Compare your results in the **Pre-viewing** activity above to your survey of the German students. How are American and German students similar or dissimilar in terms of the courses they like and dislike?

Fortsetzung

Pre-viewing

Supplementary Vocabulary			
Hast du etwas vergessen?	*Did you forget something?*	mein Zeug	*my stuff*
Batterien	*batteries*	eine Tüte	*a bag*
die Englischarbeit	*English test*	Gern geschehen!	*You're welcome!*

4. If you were Lars, what would you do next? Write your answer in these blanks.

_____

German 1 Komm mit!   Video Guide **27**

KAPITEL 4

Name _____ Klasse _____ Datum _____

 Activity Master 3

Viewing

5. Circle the correct answer or answers to each question.
   1. Was ist los mit dem Taschenrechner?
      Er ist kaputt.   Er hat keine Batterien.
   2. Wie viele Batterien kauft Lars?
      2   4
   3. Wer gibt Lars das Geld?
      Julia   Sina
   4. Was kauft Sina?
      zwei Bleistifte   drei Hefte   einen Taschenrechner
      eine Schultasche   einen Radiergummi   ein Wörterbuch
      einen Kuli   vier Kassetten   sechs Farbstifte
   5. Wann ist die Englischarbeit?
      Freitag   heute   morgen   Dienstag   nächste Woche

Post-viewing

6. How much money did Lars borrow from Julia?

_____

Videoclips: Werbung

Supplementary Vocabulary			
der Papierkorb	wastebasket	Schulranzen	book bag
Pfiff	cunning	für alle Fälle	for all situations

Viewing

7. Welche Schultasche möchtest du lieber kaufen?
   Mickey Mouse Schultaschen   Joker System Schultaschen
   Warum? _____

Post-Viewing

8. What other kinds of things do you think you could buy at **Läufer**? List them in German. Use a dictionary if necessary.

_____

_____

9. In groups of three or four compare your lists and come up with a master list. Together, pick one or two items from your list, and design an animated ad for them. Act out the ad for the class, having them try to guess which items you are portraying.

28 Video Guide   German 1 Komm mit!
Copyright © by Holt, Rinehart and Winston. All rights reserved.

KAPITEL 5 — Klamotten kaufen

Functions modeled in video:
- expressing wishes when shopping
- commenting on and describing clothes
- giving compliments and responding to them
- talking about trying on clothes

Video Segment	Correlation to Print Materials — Pupil's Edition	Video Guide — Activity Masters	Video Guide — Scripts	Videocassette 2 — Start Time	Videocassette 2 — Length	Videocassette 5 (captioned) — Start Time	Videocassette 5 (captioned) — Length
Los geht's!	pp. 130-131	p. 32	pp. 90-91	21:14	4:19	22:14	4:21
Fortsetzung		pp. 33–34	p. 91	25:35	1:37	26:36	1:36
Landeskunde	p. 142*	pp. 32, 33	pp. 91-92	27:52	5:10		
Videoclips		p. 34	p. 92	33:17	2:55		

*The *Video Program* provides film footage of the Landeskunde interviews in the *Pupil's Edition* and additional interviews.

Video Synopses

Los geht's! *Was ziehst du an?*

In this segment of the video, Katja and Julia decide to go shopping to buy something to wear to Sonja's party. At **Sport-Kerner** Katja tries on some things and finally buys a T-shirt.

Fortsetzung

Michael and Heiko also go shopping at **Sport-Kerner.** As a practical joke, they buy T-shirts like Katja's.

Landeskunde

People from different cities talk about clothes they like to wear on various occasions.

Videoclips: Werbung

1. **Quelle Katalog:** women's clothing catalog
2. **Otto Katalog:** clothing catalog
3. **Persil:** laundry detergent
4. **Hypercolor Kleidung:** sports clothes
5. **Perwoll:** laundry detergent

German 1 Komm mit! Video Guide

Teaching Suggestions

Captioned Video
Both **Los geht's!** and **Fortsetzung** are available with German captions on Videocassette 5.

Los geht's!

Pre-viewing
Ask students what they like to wear to parties. Do they generally buy new clothes for a party? Have them discuss their clothing budgets. Where do they get money for clothes?

Viewing
See **Viewing** activity on Activity Master 1, p. 32.

Post-viewing
Ask students whose T-shirt was more expensive: Katja's or Michael's? Do students understand why one T-shirt was more expensive? Ask them whether they think the price of the first Texas T-shirt was fair. Have them discuss how much they would pay for such a T-shirt.

Fortsetzung

Pre-viewing
Have students recall what happened in the **Los geht's!** section. Tell students that in the next segment of the video, Michael plays a practical joke on Katja to get even with her for making fun of his T-shirt. Have them work in groups and try to think of possible jokes he might play. If possible, have each group describe in German the joke they thought of.

Viewing
See **Viewing** activity on Activity Master 2, p. 33.

Post-viewing
Have the class compare their practical joke ideas with Michael's. Which group's was the most like Michael's? Have the class vote for the best practical joke, including Michael's.

Landeskunde

Pre-viewing
Have students put together an outfit that would be suitable for wearing to a party. Either draw the items they tell you or write them on the board, so that you have a complete list of the items in the class' "perfect" outfit.

Viewing
1. See Activity Master 1, p. 32.
2. For students to complete the clothes and color surveys on Activity Master 2, p. 33, play the **Landeskunde** part of the video twice, while students fill in the kinds of clothes that are mentioned. Then play it a third time while they fill in the favorite colors that are mentioned. Remind students to concentrate on only one survey at a time; it will be too difficult for them to try to fill in both surveys at the same time.

Post-viewing
Have students discuss the casual clothing worn by young people in this country and in German-speaking countries. Do Americans tend to dress more casually than do people from other countries? What do these interviews suggest about American influence among teenagers?

Videoclips: Werbung

Pre-viewing
Ask how many, if any, students like to read fashion magazines (for men or for women). Ask the class in general how they think such magazines influence fashion trends. Ask how many students, if any, make their own clothes, or know someone who does. Where do they get ideas for the clothes they make?

Viewing
Play the ads once without sound. Have students guess what the ads are for. Play them again, with sound, and have students confirm or correct their guesses. Play them one or two more times and have students complete the activities on Activity Master 3 on p. 34.

Post-viewing
Have groups of students write another commercial for the **Quelle** catalog.

Name _____ Klasse _____ Datum _____

Activity Master 1

Los geht's!

Supplementary Vocabulary
das Stirnband *headband*   die Baumwolle *cotton*   lässig *cool (slang)*

Viewing

1. Circle the correct answer.
   1. Was braucht Katja für die Fete?
      a. einen Jogginganzug   b. eine Bluse oder ein T-Shirt   c. Shorts oder eine Hose
   2. Wie finden Katja und Julia Michaels T-Shirt?
      a. ganz fesch   b. recht schick   c. scheußlich   d. hässlich
   3. Was kauft Katja?
      a. ein T-Shirt mit New York Motiv   c. ein T-Shirt mit Texas Motiv
      b. ein T-Shirt mit Kalifornien Motiv
   4. Wie viel kostet das T-Shirt?
      a. €12,50   b. €24,50   c. €42,00   d. €21,50

Post-viewing

2. Wie findest du Michaels T-Shirt? _____

3. Wie findest du Katjas T-Shirt? _____

Landeskunde (in *Pupil's Edition*)

Supplementary Vocabulary
der Body *body suit*   locker *loose*

Viewing

4. Below is a list of the four students who were interviewed. Beside their names is a list of colors that they like. Draw a line from each student's name to the colors that he or she mentioned.

Sandra	Blau
	Schwarz
Alexandra	Rot
	Weiß
Melina	Lila
	Apricot
Iwan	Pastellfarben

Post-viewing

5. Write in German what you normally wear to a party, then decide which of the four students interviewed has taste most similar to yours.

_____
_____

Name _____ Klasse _____ Datum _____

Activity Master 2

Landeskunde (on Video only)

Supplementary Vocabulary

andere Frisur	*a different hairdo*	der normale Alltag	*normal everyday*
einfarbig	*one-color*	das Dirndlkleid	*traditional dress of Bavaria and Austrian Alps*
die Lederjacke	*leather jacket*	die Krawatte	*necktie*

Viewing

1. To determine which items of clothing are the most popular, put a tally mark next to each kind of clothing as you hear it mentioned. As you listen a second time, draw a line connecting any colors you hear mentioned with the clothing items. For example, Gerd says that he likes to wear **ein schwarzes T-Shirt.** You should draw a line from **Schwarz** to **T-Shirt.**

   _____ Anzug
   _____ Bluse
   _____ Body
   _____ Hemd
   _____ Jacke   Blau
   _____ Jeans   Gelb
   _____ Jogginganzug   Braun
   _____ Kleid   Schwarz
   _____ Krawatte   Grau
   _____ kurze Hose   Blau
   _____ Pulli   Grün
   _____ Rock   Apricot
   _____ Shorts   Orange
   _____ Sweatshirt   Rot
   _____ T-Shirt   Lila
   _____ Turnschuhe   Weiß
   _____ Docks
   _____ Hose
   _____ Sandalen
   _____ Dirndlkleider

Post-viewing

2. Which words that you have heard for articles of clothing were probably borrowed from English? Record those words here.

   _____

3. What do you think the influence of American fashion trends on German fashion trends might be? Are there words in the interviews that support your theory?

   _____

Fortsetzung

Supplementary Vocabulary

einzigartig *unique*   Gleich zu Gleich gesellt sich gern. *Birds of a feather flock together.*

Viewing

4. Circle the correct answer or answers to these questions.
   1. Was für T-Shirts kaufen Michael und Heiko?
      a. T-Shirts mit New York Motiv   **b.** T-Shirts mit Texas Motiv   **c.** T-Shirts mit Deutschland Motiv

KAPITEL 5

German 1 Komm mit!   Video Guide **33**

Copyright © by Holt, Rinehart and Winston. All rights reserved.

Name _____ Klasse _____ Datum _____

Activity Master 3

2. Welche Farbe hat das T-Shirt?
   a. grün   b. weiß   c. blau   d. schwarz

Post-viewing

5. What does Sonja mean when she says to Katja **Du, das ist nicht das erste Mal, dass ich heute das T-Shirt sehe**?
   _____

6. How does Katja react to Michael's practical joke? _____

7. Which of these words does Katja use in her reaction?   **fesch   einzigartig   gemein**

   Judging from the way she says it, what do you think that word means? _____

8. Why do you think Michael played this joke on Katja? _____

Videoclips: Werbung

Supplementary Vocabulary
Seidenblousons *silk jackets*   Weichpfleger *fabric softener*   Schmusewolle *soft wool*

Viewing

9. Put a check mark under **stimmt** or **stimmt nicht** to indicate whether the following statements are correct or not. If a statement is not correct, restate it correctly in the blank provided.

                                                                                stimmt   stimmt nicht

   1. In **Werbung 1** sucht die Frau Richard. _____   _____   _____

   2. Der Mann heißt Richard. _____   _____   _____

   3. In **Werbung 5** ist die Bluse neu. _____   _____   _____

Post-viewing

10. Imagine that you and your partner are consultants for an advertising agency. You like the way **Werbung 1** (the commercial for the **Quelle** catalog) looks, but you want them to say something else. Write a new text for this ad.
    _____
    _____
    _____

11. With a partner, create a conversation that might have taken place between the farmer and his well-dressed cow.

KAPITEL 5

KAPITEL 6: Pläne machen

Functions modeled in video:
- starting a conversation
- telling time and talking about when you do things
- making plans
- ordering food and beverages
- talking about how something tastes
- paying the check

Video Segment	Correlation to Print Materials			Videocassette 2		Videocassette 5 (captioned)	
	Pupil's Edition	Video Guide Activity Masters	Scripts	Start Time	Length	Start Time	Length
Los geht's!	pp. 158–159	p. 38	p. 93	36:30	4:12	28:19	4:12
Fortsetzung		pp. 39–40	p. 93	40:45	1:57	32:34	1:56
Landeskunde	p. 169*	pp. 38, 39	pp. 93-95	43:20	5:28		
Videoclips		p. 40	p. 95	49:02	2:00		

*The *Video Program* provides film footage of the Landeskunde interviews in the *Pupil's Edition* and additional interviews.

Video Synopses

Los geht's! *Wollen wir ins Café gehen?*

In this segment of the video, several friends (Julia, Katja, Heiko, and Michael) meet at **Café Freizeit** for a bite to eat. As Michael is getting up to leave, he accidentally spills his drink on Katja's new T-shirt.

Fortsetzung

The scene at **Café Freizeit** continues as Heiko has something to eat and the girls have a mineral water. Michael returns with an apology for staining Katja's T-shirt.

Landeskunde

People of various ages from different cities talk about what they do in their free time.

Videoclips: Werbung

1. **Junghans:** watches
2. **Wagner-Pizza:** pizza
3. **Sacher Eis:** ice cream
4. **Überkinger Mineralwasser:** mineral water

German 1 Komm mit!

Teaching Suggestions

Captioned Video
Both **Los geht's!** and **Fortsetzung** are available with German captions on Videocassette 5.

Los geht's!

Pre-viewing
Ask students what they do after school. Do a class survey: Where do the students in your class go after school to get something to eat, if anywhere? Ask them about the most popular places to go near the school. Ask them what they like to eat and drink at these places.

Viewing
While watching the video, have students use the **Viewing** activity on Activity Master 1, p. 38 to jot down what each of the students in the video segment orders.

Post-viewing
Have students pick which of the things ordered by Julia, Michael, Heiko, and Katja they would have ordered. Have them say whether they like each food and beverage or not.

Fortsetzung

Pre-viewing
Have students discuss how both Michael and Katja might have felt after Michael spilled his cola on Katja. Have them tell you what reaction they might expect from Katja and what they might do next in both Michael's and Katja's cases.

Viewing
Have students record what Heiko, Katja, and Julia order. Ask students to be prepared to describe what Michael does in this act, and why they think he does it.

Post-viewing
Ask students to describe what Michael did, and why they think he did it. Ask them if his actions had the desired effect or not.

Landeskunde

Pre-viewing
Have students write down their favorite free-time activities on a slip of paper, without including their names. Collect the papers, then hand them out randomly. Have students find the authors of their papers by asking **Was machst du gern in deiner Freizeit?** or **Spielst du Fußball/ Basketball/Klavier/usw.?**

Viewing
1. Have students do the **Viewing** activity on Activity Master 1, p. 38.
2. Give your students a list of all the students who are interviewed, then have them write beside each name the activities that person mentioned. Have them do the **Viewing** activity on Activity Master 2, p. 39.

Post-viewing
1. Have students study the list and pick out the person or people with whom they would most likely want to be friends, based on common interests.
2. Have students write a letter introducing themselves to the persons they picked out as potential friends. Have them include in their letter reasons why they think those persons would make good friends.

Videoclips: Werbung

Pre-viewing
Write the names of several kinds of food items (ice cream bars, tea, cola, frozen microwavable snacks, etc.) on slips of paper, and hand them out to groups of three or four students. Have each group think of a name for their product, then write an ad for it. Have them perform their ads for the rest of the class, and have the class guess what the product is.

Viewing
Tell students as they watch the ads to imagine that they are craving a snack after school. Tell them to select one of the products advertised (but only one!) and be prepared to tell the class why they want that product as a snack.

Post-viewing
Have students report what they decided to eat and/or drink, and say why.

Name _____ Klasse _____ Datum _____

Activity Master 1

Los geht's!

Viewing

1. Wann gehen Julia, Katja und Heiko ins Café?

   Supplementary Vocabulary
   der Haarschnitt   *haircut*   gar nichts   *nothing at all*

   1. 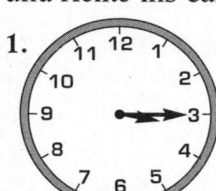   2.    3. 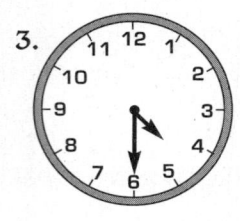   4.

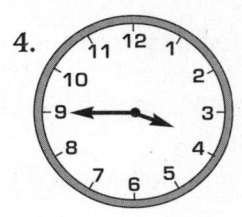

2. Match each person with the food item that he or she ordered.
   _____ 1. Heiko
   _____ 2. Katja
   _____ 3. Julia
   _____ 4. Michael

   a.    b.    c. 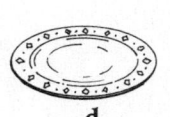   d.

Post-viewing

3. 1. Was sagt Katja zu Michael?
      a. Man ist, was man ist, mein lieber Michael.
      b. Man ist, was man isst, mein lieber Michael.
      c. Du bist nicht, was du isst, mein lieber Michael.

   2. What is the closest English equivalent to Katja's statement?
      a. You are what you are, my dear Michael.
      b. You are what you eat, my dear Michael.
      c. You are not what you eat, my dear Michael.

   3. Do you agree with Katja's statement? Why or why not?
      _____
      _____

Landeskunde (in *Pupil's Edition*)

Viewing

4. Match the person with the activity you hear that person mention.

   Supplementary Vocabulary
   die Pfadfinder   *girl/boy scouts*

   _____ 1. Sandra
   _____ 2. Annika
   _____ 3. Marga
   _____ 4. Karsten

   a.    b.   c.    d.

38   Video Guide   German 1 Komm mit!

Name _____ Klasse _____ Datum _____

Activity Master 2

Landeskunde (on Video only)

Supplementary Vocabulary

proben	rehearse	Wir versammeln uns …	We gather…
ein Zeitvertreib	pastime	Bei mir läuft's gleich ab.	It's the same with me.
der Schiedsrichter	referee	abwechslungsreich	varied
beanspruchen	to make demands	zurechtkommen	to deal with/come to terms with
Es lohnt sich nicht.	It's not worth it.		

Viewing

1. Keep a tally of how many people mention the various activities listed below.

   _____ Hausaufgaben   _____ Arbeit (*work*)   _____ Sport
   _____ Klubs   _____ Musik   _____ mit Freunden etwas
   _____ essen/trinken   _____ ins Kino gehen   unternehmen
   _____ in eine Disco gehen/tanzen   _____ ins Theater gehen

Post-viewing

2. Based on your tally above, name the three types of activities that are most popular among German students.
   _____

3. If you did interviews with several students in your area, would you predict similar results? Why or why not?
   _____
   _____

Fortsetzung

Viewing

4. Put a check mark in the appropriate column to indicate whether the following statements are true or false based on what you hear in the video.

   Supplementary Vocabulary

waschen	to wash	der Fleck	stain
rausgehen	to go out	sauer sein	to be annoyed/angry

	stimmt	stimmt nicht
1. Der Fleck von dem Cola geht bestimmt nicht raus.	_____	_____
2. Heiko bestellt die Nudelsuppe.	_____	_____
3. Julia und Katja bestellen ein Cola.	_____	_____
4. Katja findet den Kellner sehr nett.	_____	_____
5. Julia meint, der Kellner sieht nicht gut aus.	_____	_____
6. Michael gibt Katja ein T-Shirt, genau wie sein T-Shirt.	_____	_____
7. Katja ist jetzt wirklich sauer.	_____	_____

KAPITEL 6

German 1 Komm mit!   Video Guide **39**

Name _____ Klasse _____ Datum _____

Activity Master 3

Post-viewing

5. What did Michael do to make up for his clumsiness? _____

   Was Katja appeased by his actions? _____

   How do you know? _____

   Can you remember what she said to him? _____

Videoclips: Werbung

Viewing

6. In which order are the commercials presented?

   _____ Überkinger
   _____ Sacher
   _____ Junghans
   _____ Wagner

Supplementary Vocabulary	
die Funkuhr	radio watch
funkgesteuert	radio-controlled
die Sommerzeit	daylight savings time
die Winterzeit	standard time
der Steinbackofen	brick oven

7. Match the brand names with the type of product advertised.

   _____ 1. Sacher   a. pizza
   _____ 2. Überkinger   b. watches
   _____ 3. Wagner   c. ice cream
   _____ 4. Junghans   d. mineral water

Post-viewing

8. After watching the video, write what you think each of the phrases used with these products means.

   1. Junghans: Uhren mit Ideen _____

   2. Einmal Wagner, immer Wagner! _____

   3. Sacher — der Anfang einer großen Leidenschaft! _____

   4. Überkinger: Spür die Kraft der Mineralien! _____

9. Working with a partner, pick one of the four commercials in this chapter and write an ad for that product that would be appropriate for a magazine. In what type of magazine would you expect to see an ad like the one you and your partner create?

KAPITEL 6

40 Video Guide   German 1 Komm mit!

Location Opener for Chapters 7-9

Location: München

Start Time: 1:14
Length: 3:54
Student textbook pp. 190-191

The language in this location opener is authentic German spoken at a normal rate and may be difficult for students to understand. It should be made clear to them that they are not expected to understand everything. The types of activities you choose to do with them should be designed to help them understand the major points; the activities included for this section have been designed with this in mind. (script on p. 95)

Teaching Suggestions

Pre-viewing

1. Have students locate Munich on the map on p. 185 or on p. 2 of their textbooks. Have them tell you in what state Munich is located and the names of the states that border it. Have them look at the photos on pp. 184-185 and tell you their impression of Munich.

2. Go through pp. 186-187 of the *Pupil's Edition* with the students. Use the information in the *Teacher's Edition* on pp. 183A-183B to provide background information about Munich and Bavaria in general.

3. Before showing the Location Opener, ask students to watch it with the following questions in mind: What clues in the photos give them information about the type of city Munich is and the kinds of events that take place there? Based on these impressions, what kind of city do they think Munich is? Old? Modern? Traditional? Have them explain their impressions.

Viewing

Step 1 Show the video once without sound and discuss with the class the answers to the above questions about Munich. They may not have enough information to answer them yet, but they will get more information each time they view the segment.

Step 2 Show the video again without sound, having students write the major attractions they see in the order they see them. (Let them use simple answers at this point, such as *building* or *marketplace,* as long as they accurately convey what is in the photo.)

Step 3 Help students work their way through the Supplementary Vocabulary on the Activity Master. Help students see that they can make intelligent guesses about meaning by looking for cognates.

Step 4 Have students read along as you pronounce the names of the places described in activity 1 and activity 2 on p. 42. This will help students to correlate the written German with the spoken German as they complete the activities.

Step 5 Show the video with sound, and have students complete the Location Opener activities on p. 42.

Post-viewing

1. Have students, working either in pairs or groups, compare their answers on the Activity Master. Play the video once again, if necessary.

2. Make statements and have students say whether they are correct (**stimmt**) or incorrect (**stimmt nicht**), for example, **Auf dem Viktualienmarkt kann man frisches Obst und Gemüse kaufen. (stimmt)** or **Das Reepschlägerhaus ist ein Wahrzeichen von München. (stimmt nicht — ... von Wedel.)** Have them correct statements that are false.

3. Go back to the general questions about Munich you posed before viewing and discuss the answers. Have students defend their answers by referring to what they saw in the video. Lead students into a discussion of some cultural issues by asking the following questions: Do you think Munich has a lot of tradition? Is it an important city in Germany's history?

German 1 Komm mit!

Name _____ Klasse _____ Datum _____

Activity Master: Location Opener

Supplementary Vocabulary

die Hauptstadt	capital city	der Bayrische Landtag	Bavarian state legislature (building)
das Gebäude	building		
der Blick	view	die Landesregierung	state government
die Kirche	church	der Dom	cathedral
der Turm	tower	das Herz	heart
die gute Stube	living room	der Techniker	technician/engineer
der Künstler	artist	das Kunstmuseum	art museum
der Kurfürst	elector	der Fußgänger	pedestrian
Radler	cyclist	die Lebensmittel	groceries
das Münchner Kindl	the Munich child (symbol for Munich)		
stattfinden/stattgefunden	to take place/took place		

Viewing

1. Circle the word or phrase that best completes the sentence according to what Mara says.
   1. Die Staatskanzelei der Landesregierung ist *alt / neu*.
   2. Der Dom hat *drei / zwei* Türme.
   3. Die Figuren im Glockenspiel zeigen Szenen aus der bayrischen *Landschaft / Geschichte*.
   4. In der Alten Pinakothek sind Kunstwerke aus dem *12.-17. Jahrhundert / 14.-18. Jahrhundert*.
   5. Schloss Nymphenburg war die Sommerresidenz von *französischen / bayrischen* Kurfürsten und Prinzen.
   6. Der Viktualienmarkt ist der älteste und größte Lebensmittelmarkt *in Deutschland / in München*.

2. Match each museum with what Mara says about it.
   _____ 1. Deutsches Museum   a. hat Meister aus dem 19. Jahrhundert
   _____ 2. Alte Pinakothek   b. für Techniker
   _____ 3. Neue Pinakothek   c. für Autofreaks
   _____ 4. BMW-Museum   d. hat Meister aus dem 14.-18. Jahrhundert

Post-viewing

3. Which of the museums above would you most like to visit? Why? What would you like to see there? Write your answers below.

   _____
   _____

4. Try to find the answers to these questions as you watch the Location Opener segment. Circle the correct answers.
   1. München ist die Hauptstadt von
      Schleswig-Holstein   Brandenburg   Bayern
   2. Was kann man alles auf dem Marienplatz machen?
      Tennis spielen   ein Buch lesen   essen
      tanzen   Briefmarken sammeln   auf Freunde warten
   3. Was sind die Wahrzeichen Münchens?
      Schloss Sanssouci   der Anker   das Hexenwegle
      der Viktualienmarkt   das Münchner Kindl   der Roland
      der Dom   das Brandenburger Tor
   4. Was ist der Viktualienmarkt?
      ein großer Park   der älteste Lebensmittelmarkt in München
      ein großer Blumenmarkt   eine Fußgängerzone

42 Video Guide

German 1 Komm mit!

Copyright © by Holt, Rinehart and Winston. All rights reserved.

KAPITEL 7 Zu Hause helfen

Functions modeled in video:
- extending and responding to an invitation
- expressing obligations
- talking about how often you have to do things
- asking for and offering help, and telling someone what to do
- talking about the weather

Video Segment	Correlation to Print Materials			Videocassette 3		Videocassette 5 (captioned)	
	Pupil's Edition	Video Guide				
		Activity Masters	Scripts	Start Time	Length	Start Time	Length
Los geht's!	pp. 190-191	p. 46	p. 96	5:10	3:24	34:37	3:00
Fortsetzung		pp. 47-48	p. 96	8:36	4:02	37:39	4:24
Landeskunde	p. 197*	pp. 46, 47	pp. 96-98	13:16	6:33		
Videoclips		p. 48	p. 98	20:03	3:57		

*The *Video Program* provides film footage of the Landeskunde interviews in the *Pupil's Edition* and additional interviews.

Video Synopses

Los geht's! *Was musst du machen?*

In this segment of the video, Mara, Flori, and Markus invite Claudia to go bike riding with them in the **Englischer Garten**. Claudia declines their invitation because she has to do some work at home. The friends end up helping Claudia with her chores.

Fortsetzung

Flori found the cat and is in the kitchen feeding her. Flori's mother calls and tells Flori that he, too, has chores that have to be done. The whole group goes to Flori's and helps him with his housework. When they have finished, Flori's mother sends them off to the **Englischer Garten** with a picnic basket filled with goodies.

Landeskunde

People from different cities talk about what they and their communities do for the environment.

Videoclips: Wetterbericht

This is an actual weather report from the TV news.

Videoclips: Werbung

1. **HK Selbstbausystem:** do-it-yourself closets and shelves
2. **Siemens:** vacuum cleaner
3. **Der General:** kitchen cleaner
4. **Dixan:** laundry detergent
5. **AL-KO Ökostar:** lawnmower

German 1 Komm mit!   Video Guide **43**

Teaching Suggestions

Captioned Video
Both **Los geht's!** and **Fortsetzung** are available with German captions on Videocassette 5.

Los geht's!

Pre-viewing
Ask students what they have to do at home to help out. Make a survey of their tasks (provide additional vocabulary as necessary, or have them look up additional vocabulary in a dictionary). Leave this list up on the board while students view the video.

Viewing
Have students write down the names of Claudia's friends (Mara, Markus, and Flori). As they listen to the **Los geht's!** video segment, have them write each person's task at Claudia's house beside that person's name.

Post-viewing
Have students compare the list on the board with the list from the video. Is there anything missing from either list? If so, what is it? See if students can draw any conclusions about similarities or differences between chores that American teenagers have to do and chores that German teenagers have to do.

Fortsetzung

Pre-viewing
Find out how many people in the class have cats or other pets. Find out which family member is responsible for feeding the pet. (This is a good opportunity to recycle family vocabulary: **Wer füttert die Katze? Dein Bruder? Deine Mutter?**)

Viewing
Have students make a list of the things Flori's friends do to help him.

Post-viewing
Have students first list in German the chores that were done at Claudia's house. Then have them compare those chores with those that were done at Flori's. Were there any chores done at one place that were not mentioned at the other? Have them compare those chores to those listed on the board in the **Pre-viewing** activity above.

Landeskunde

Pre-viewing
Have students rate themselves on a scale of 1 - 10, where 1 = no concern about the environment, and 10 = completely committed to activities that help save the environment. Have them tell you what they do to help the environment.

Viewing
Have students listen carefully to each interview and write down the name of the person interviewed whose environmental habits are the closest to their own.

Post-viewing
1. As a follow-up to the **Viewing** activity on p. 47 (the rating scale), have students compare their ratings among themselves. Do most of them agree, or are there considerable differences of opinion? Have students discuss their ratings in groups, using as much German as possible.
2. Go through the class and have students say which name they wrote down, then group students together based on their common answers (for example, all the people who wrote down Marga form one group). Have the groups compare how they rated themselves during the **Pre-viewing** activity, then use the same scale to rate the person from the video whom they selected. Have them tell the rest of the group what they do or do not do for the environment.

Videoclips: Wetterbericht

Pre-viewing
Ask students to describe the weather today; on a typical summer day; in the middle of winter.

Viewing
Have students tell you what season it is when the weather report is given. Have them tell you any words or phrases they remember that gave them information about the season.

Post-viewing
Have students pair up and write weather reports for your area. Assign different times of year to each pair. Have them perform their weather reports for the class. If possible, videotape the performances. Have those not performing guess in what season the report is given.

Videoclips: Werbung

Pre-viewing
Have students list things they might see advertised that could help them with chores around the house.

Viewing
Play the ads without sound and have students identify the products advertised. Then play the ads with sound, and have students do the **Viewing** activities on Activity Master 3, p. 48.

Post-viewing
Have students write short skits in groups of two or three in which one of the students is a traveling salesperson selling one of the products in the ads, and the others are persons who answer the door to the salesperson. Some like the product and want to buy it, but some don't!

Name _____ Klasse _____ Datum _____

Activity Master 1

Los geht's!

Supplementary Vocabulary	
füttern *to feed*	sowieso *anyway*

Viewing

1. As you watch the video, determine who does each chore pictured here. Write the name of the person in the blank under the drawing.

a. _____   b. _____   c. _____

Post-viewing

2. Answer these questions about what you saw in this video segment.

   1. Where do Claudia's friends want her to go with them? _____
   2. What reason does she give for not being able to go? _____
   3. Who offers a solution to the problem? _____
   4. What chore does Mara always have to do at home? _____
   5. At the end of the segment, are the friends ready to go to the **Englischer Garten**? _____

      If not, why not? _____

Landeskunde (in *Pupil's Edition*)

Supplementary Vocabulary			
streng einhalten	*to stick to something very strictly*	fortschrittlich	*progressive/advanced*
vermeiden	*to avoid*	wieder verwerten	*here: to recycle*
umweltbewusst	*environmentally aware*	der Abguss	*sink, drain*
das Putzmittel	*cleaning agent*		

Viewing

3. Listen to what each student says, then match each person with the statement that he or she is most likely to say.

   1. Marga   a. Wir sammeln Glas und Altpapier und bringen sie weg.
   2. Fabian   b. Wenn das Wetter schön ist, dann fahre ich lieber mit dem Fahrrad.
   3. Elke   c. Wir sortieren den Müll und bringen ihn regelmäßig zum Container.

46 Video Guide   German 1 Komm mit!

Name _____ Klasse _____ Datum _____

Activity Master 2

Landeskunde (on Video only)

Supplementary Vocabulary			
durchschnittlich	average	der Wasserverbrauch	water consumption
der Energieverbrauch	energy consumption	der Abfall = der Müll	
die Tonne	container	sparen	to save
der Strom	electricity	kompostieren	to compost
umweltfreundlich	concerned about the environment	der Trabi	a small car built in former East Germany
die Luft verpesten	to pollute the air	verzichten	to do without
der Kunststoff	artificial materials, such as plastic	einführen	to introduce
gesondert	separated	sammeln	to gather/collect

KAPITEL 7

Viewing

1. In this **Landeskunde** several people were asked what they do for the environment. Rate them on a scale of 1 to 5, where 1 indicates the least amount of environmental involvement and 5 means very environmentally aware. Note: listen not only to what they say, but how they say it: do they seem enthusiastic about or a little bored with environmental issues?

   Margit   1 2 3 4 5   Johannes   1 2 3 4 5   Ria   1 2 3 4 5
   Susanne   1 2 3 4 5   Marco   1 2 3 4 5   Jens   1 2 3 4 5
   Herr Troger 1 2 3 4 5   Sandra   1 2 3 4 5   Jutta 1 2 3 4 5
   Ute   1 2 3 4 5   Alexandra 1 2 3 4 5   Silke 1 2 3 4 5
   Rolf   1 2 3 4 5   Eva   1 2 3 4 5

Post-viewing

2. Listen to the **Landeskunde** again, then complete these statements by supplying the appropriate word or phrase.

   Abfall   sparen   Energieverbrauch   umweltfreundliche   Tonne   kompostiert   die Luft verpesten

   1. JENS   Ich mag die Autos nicht, die _____ .
   2. MARGIT   Ich trenne meinen _____ so weit wie möglich, also Papier, Alu, Glas, usw.
   3. SANDRA   Bei uns wird im Garten alles _____ .
   4. RIA   Wir benutzen zu Hause nur _____ Putzmittel.
   5. JOHANNES   Wir versuchen (*try*), Wasser zu _____ — nicht so viel zu verbrauchen.
   6. HERR TROGER Also, der Hausmüll kommt in eine _____ und wird weggebracht.

Fortsetzung

Viewing

3. Mark the following statements as true (**stimmt**) or false (**stimmt nicht**). If the statement is false, restate it correctly.

	stimmt	stimmt nicht
1. Florian isst Katzenfutter.	_____	_____ (_____)

German 1 Komm mit! Video Guide **47**

Name _____ Klasse _____ Datum _____

Activity Master 3

2. Florian muss nach Hause gehen und arbeiten. ____ ____ (____)
3. Florian mäht den Rasen. ____ ____ (____)
4. Florian gießt die Blumen. ____ ____ (____)
5. Markus begießt Florian mit Wasser. ____ ____ (____)
6. Markus, Claudia, Mara und Florian machen endlich ein Picknick. ____ ____ (____)

Videoclips: Wetterbericht

Supplementary Vocabulary

die Abwechslung	change	die Aufheiterung	improvement in the weather
der Schneefall	snowfall	die Flockentreibung	snow flurries
feucht	damp		

4. Answer these questions about the weather report.
   1. Welche Jahreszeit ist es? _____
   2. Wo ist es in Deutschland am kältesten? _____
   3. Wo scheint die Sonne in Europa? _____

Videoclips: Werbung

Supplementary Vocabulary

überall passend	fits in everywhere	unerhört variabel	remarkably variable
ohne Nachwischen	without rinsing	streifenfrei	without streaking
alles glänzend sauber	everything sparkling clean	Anti-Kalkformel	anti-calcium formula
unverschämt preiswert	unashamedly reasonably priced (a great bargain!)		
der Kalk im Wasser	calcium in the water (hard water)		
das Umweltbewusstsein	environmental consciousness/awareness		

Viewing

5. Match the brand names with the activities for which the products are used.
   ___ 1. HK   a. alles in Ordnung bringen
   ___ 2. Siemens   b. die Küche putzen
   ___ 3. Der General c. den Rasen mähen
   ___ 4. Dixan 2000   d. Staub saugen
   ___ 5. AL-KO Ökostar e. Klamotten waschen

Post-viewing

6. Working with a partner, create a flyer for a store in which you advertise each of the products featured in the video.

KAPITEL 8: Einkaufen gehen

Functions modeled in video:
- asking what you should do
- telling someone what to do
- talking about quantities
- saying that you want something else
- giving reasons
- saying where you were and what you bought

Video Segment	Correlation to Print Materials			Videocassette 3		Videocassette 5 (captioned)	
	Pupil's Edition	Video Guide		Start Time	Length	Start Time	Length
		Activity Masters	Scripts				
Los geht's!	pp. 218-219	p. 52	pp. 98-99	24:15	4:15	42:10	4:17
Fortsetzung		p. 53	p. 99	28:35	2:37	46:28	2:38
Landeskunde	p. 225*	pp. 52, 53	pp. 99-100	31:51	1:31		
Videoclips		p. 54	p. 100	33:37	3:03		

*The *Video Program* provides film footage of the Landeskunde interviews in the *Pupil's Edition* and additional interviews.

Video Synopses

Los geht's! *Alles für die Oma!*

In this segment of the video, Flori visits his grandmother, who has cooked one of his favorite dishes, **Kaiserschmarren**. After lunch, Flori's grandmother gives him a shopping list and some money to go shopping for her. After going to several specialty stores on his errands, Flori comes back to his grandmother's house but discovers that he has lost the wallet she had given him.

Fortsetzung

Flori asks the florist if she has found his wallet, but it isn't there. He bumps into Claudia and Mara, who are going shopping. Flori calls his grandmother to tell her that he is going with Claudia and Mara and learns from his grandmother that she has found the wallet. The three of them continue through the open-air market and Claudia buys various fruits and vegetables. The scene closes with Mara, Claudia, and Flori walking through the market, eating peaches.

Landeskunde

Young people from different cities talk about what they do to help other people.

Videoclips: Werbung

1. **Nuß-Nougat Brötchen:** rolls
2. **Weihenstephan:** dairy products
3. **Milram Frucht Quark:** quark
4. **Gerolsteiner Stille Quelle:** mineral water
5. **Sonnen-Bassermann:** canned stew
6. **Gutfried Wurst:** cold cuts
7. **CMA Gütezeichen:** quality control symbol

German 1 Komm mit! Video Guide

Teaching Suggestions

Captioned Video
Both **Los geht's!** and **Fortsetzung** are available with German captions on Videocassette 5.

Los geht's!

Pre-viewing
Ask students if they ever do the shopping for or with other members of their family. Where do they go to buy the various items they need? How often do they go, and how much money do they usually spend in one shopping trip? Less or more than $20.00? Do they buy all the groceries at a supermarket, or do they sometimes go to a bakery or butcher shop?

Viewing
While watching the video, have students make a list of the things Flori buys for his grandmother.

Post-viewing
Have students work in pairs and act out the following situation. One student in the group is Flori, the others are the sale personnel at the bakery, the butcher's, and the florist's. Have them buy and sell the things that are on Flori's list.

Fortsetzung

Pre-viewing
Have students tell you what they would do in Flori's case—if they came back from shopping and couldn't find their wallet. Have them predict what Flori will do.

Viewing
Have students make a list of the things Claudia buys at the market.

Post-viewing
Have students play the role of Claudia and the woman at the market and have them make the purchases Claudia makes. (You might want to add props, including fruit, vegetables, a table, and perhaps a scale to weigh out a kilo of tomatoes.) Or: Have students create and act out the phone conversation that might have taken place between Flori and his grandmother if neither of them had found the wallet.

Landeskunde

Pre-viewing
Ask students what they do to help other people, and let them respond in English. Write key words on the board and have students come up with the German equivalents of those terms. Have them work in groups and use a dictionary if needed to generate a list of words and phrases that express chores and obligations.

Viewing
Have students make a list of the activities they hear that these four students do for other people. They should write down each activity, even if they do not understand all the words or don't know how to spell the ones they hear. You may have to play the video several times in order for them to get all the activities.

Post-viewing
Have students get into groups and compare their lists. Have them look up the words they were unsure of or did not know how to spell. Have them compare the lists they generated in the **Pre-viewing** activity with the list they made while watching the video. What similarities or differences did they find between what American students do to help others and what German students do?

Videoclips: Werbung

Pre-viewing
Tell students what **Quark** is (a soft white cheese, similar to cottage cheese but without curds) and how in German-speaking countries there seems to be a much greater variety of dairy products than is available in the United States. If you have any labels from German dairy products, such as **Quark,** bring them and show them to the class at this time.

Viewing
See **Viewing** activities on Activity Master 3, page 54.

Post-viewing
Have students work in groups. Assign each group a product from the **Werbung: Joghurt, Quark,** etc. Have each group make up a brand name for their product and write and perform a commercial for the product.

Name _____ Klasse _____ Datum _____

Activity Master 1

Los geht's!

Supplementary Vocabulary

der Einkaufszettel	shopping list	verlieren	to lose
aufpassen	to pay attention, be careful	das Portemonnaie	wallet
die Brezenstange	pretzel stick		

Viewing

1. Place a check mark beside the stores that Flori goes to while he is shopping for his grandmother.

   _____ 1. Obst- und Gemüseladen   _____ 5. Metzger
   _____ 2. Supermarkt   _____ 6. Apotheke
   _____ 3. Schreibwarenladen   _____ 7. Blumenladen
   _____ 4. Bäckerei

2. Circle the correct answer to these questions.
   1. Wie viel Aufschnitt kauft Flori?   **a.** 10 Gramm   **b.** 100 Gramm   **c.** 500 Gramm
   2. Wie viele Brote kauft er?   **a.** 1   **b.** 2   **c.** 3
   3. Wie viele Semmeln kauft er?   **a.** 1   **b.** 2   **c.** 3
   4. Wie viele Brezeln kauft er?   **a.** 1   **b.** 2   **c.** 3

Post-viewing

3. You are planning to have a Sunday brunch for three of your friends. You want to serve omelettes with cheese and vegetables, as well as fresh fruit and salad. You will also serve rolls or bread on the side. Your partner has offered to do the shopping for you. Working with him or her, make a list of everything you will need in order to serve the above meal to three friends. Discuss where your partner will need to go to buy everything. Be sure to include quantities.

_____
_____
_____

Landeskunde (in *Pupil's Edition*)

Viewing

4. The teenagers in this **Landeskunde** segment were asked what they do to help other people. Each statement below summarizes what one of the teenagers in the video said. Complete each one with the correct name.

Supplementary Vocabulary

die Gesellschaft	company/companionship
die Kinderkirche	children's church/Sunday School
unregelmäßig	irregularly
die Nachhilfe	tutoring

1. _____ hilft in einer Kinderkirche und spielt dort mit Kindern.
2. _____ hilft einem kleinen Schüler zweimal in der Woche mit Rechtschreiben, Lesen und Mathe.
3. _____ hilft seinem Bruder, wenn er Probleme in der Schule hat, und seiner Oma, wenn er zu ihr geht.
4. _____ geht für eine ältere Nachbarin manchmal einkaufen und redet mit ihr, damit sie nicht so allein ist.

KAPITEL 8

52 Video Guide   German 1 Komm mit!

Copyright © by Holt, Rinehart and Winston. All rights reserved.

Name _____ Klasse _____ Datum _____

Activity Master 2

Landeskunde (in *Pupil's Edition*)

Post-viewing

1. Listen to each of the students and complete the statements below with the words and/or expressions from the box.

   | *Gesellschaft* | *unregelmäßig* | *Nachhilfe* | *Kinderkirche* |
   | *Rechtschreibung* | *Nachbarschaft* | *langweilig* |

   1. Zweimal in der Woche gebe ich _____ .

   2. Dem Schüler gebe ich Unterricht in Lesen, Mathematik und _____ .

   3. Bei uns in der _____ wohnt eine ältere Frau.

   4. Ich versuche, ihr _____ zu leisten, damit es ihr nicht so _____ ist.

   5. Sonntags habe ich mit den Kindern _____ , aber ich mache das _____ .

Fortsetzung

Supplementary Vocabulary			
der Geldbeutel	*coin purse*	die Gurke	*cucumber*
der Pfirsich	*peach*	saftig	*juicy*
lecker	*tasty, delicious*		

Viewing

2. ____ Wer findet den Geldbeutel?
   a. Flori   b. Floris Oma   c. Claudia   d. Mara

3. Write in the amounts of the things Claudia buys.

   _____ Tomaten

   _____ Kirschen

   _____ Gurken

   _____ Salat

   _____ Pfirsiche

4. How does the woman at the market describe the peaches?

   _____

KAPITEL 8

German 1 Komm mit!   Video Guide **53**

Name _____ Klasse _____ Datum _____

Activity Master 3

Videoclips: Werbung

Supplementary vocabulary

der Konditor	*pastry shop*	das Fruchthäubchen	*fruit topping*
etwas Köstliches	*something exquisite, delicious*	der Eintopf	*stew/casserole*
Kontrollierte Qualität bringt Sicherheit.	*Controlled quality results in confidence.*		

Viewing

5. Match the brand names with the type of product advertised.

   _____ 1. Weihenstephan   a. stew
   _____ 2. Gerolsteiner   b. mineral water
   _____ 3. Milram   c. cold cuts
   _____ 4. Sonnen-Bassermann   d. symbol of quality
   _____ 5. CMA   e. yogurt
   _____ 6. Gutfried   f. roll
   _____ 7. Nuß-Nougat Brötchen g. quark (soft cheese)

6. Now match each product advertised with a statement made about the product.

   1. Nuß-Nougat Brötchen   a. ... hat frische Gemüse.
   2. Weihenstephan Joghurt   b. kontrollierte Qualität.
   3. Milram Fruchtquark   c. Als wär' er selbst gemacht!
   4. Sonnen-Bassermann Suppe   d. Bei ihrem Bäcker oder Konditor!
   5. Gerolsteiner Stille Quelle e. Sie ist gut für mich.
   6. Gutfried-Wurst   f. Köstliches aus Milch!
   7. CMA Gütezeichen   g. Still, mit viel Charakter.

Post-viewing

7. Working with a partner, pick one of the products from the commercials in this chapter and write a "celebrity" ad for that product—an ad in which some well-known person does a commercial for your product (preferably a well-known German-speaking person). Act out your commercial for the rest of the class.

KAPITEL 9: Amerikaner in München

Functions modeled in video:
- talking about where something is located
- asking for and giving directions
- talking about what there is to eat and drink
- saying you do or don't want more
- expressing opinions

Video Segment	Correlation to Print Materials			Videocassette 3		Videocassette 5 (captioned)	
	Pupil's Edition	Video Guide					
		Activity Masters	Scripts	Start Time	Length	Start Time	Length
Los geht's!	pp. 246-247	p. 58	pp. 100-101	36:50	2:20	49:13	2:15
Fortsetzung		p. 60	p. 101	39:14	3:34	51:30	3:35
Landeskunde	p. 252*	pp. 58, 59	pp. 101-102	43:13	5:49		
Videoclips		p. 60	p. 102	49:29	3:19		

*The *Video Program* provides film footage of the Landeskunde interviews in the *Pupil's Edition* and additional interviews.

Video Synopses

Los geht's! *München besuchen*

In this segment of the video, Mara and Markus are having some juice at a juice bar when some American students ask them for directions to the **Marienplatz**. They run into each other again at an **Imbissstube** later in the day. Markus and Mara talk the Americans into trying a Bavarian specialty, **Leberkäs**, and then decide to show them around Munich.

Fortsetzung

Mara, Markus, and the Americans see different sights in **München**, and Mara explains what they are seeing. When it is time for the Americans to get back to Rosenheim, Markus and Mara give them directions to the U-Bahn which will take them to the train station. At the **U-Bahn** station, Mara gives them an **U-Bahn** ticket and tells them how to validate it.

Landeskunde

People of various ages from different cities talk about what they like to eat.

Videoclips: Werbung

1. **Siemens Museum:** museum
2. **Nordsee:** fast food
3. **Postbank:** banking by mail
4. **Postbank:** business by mail

Teaching Suggestions

Captioned Video
Both **Los geht's!** and **Fortsetzung** are available with German captions on Videocassette 5.

Los geht's!

Pre-viewing
Have students tell you about any experiences they may have had visiting a large city or a foreign country. How did they get around? How did they find places? Did they try any specialties from that city or country?

Viewing
See **Viewing** activity on Activity Master 1, p. 58.

Post-viewing
Note: For this activity, students will need to know directions such as left, right, and straight ahead (see *Pupil's Edition*, p. 253). If you do this activity early in the chapter, it would be good review to return to it after students have been through the chapter.

Write several locations in your area on cards or slips of paper (the library, the museum, the post-office, etc.), and distribute them to your students. Have the students pair up. Student A asks B how to get to the location on his or her (A's) card. B gives directions. The students then reverse roles.

Fortsetzung

Pre-viewing
Have students make plans for an imaginary group of German teenagers who will visit your school soon. Your students will be their hosts and need to plan where they will go, what they will see, and what activities they will do.

Viewing
Play the video once without sound and have students write down the places Mara and Markus take the Americans to see. Play it again with sound and have them complete the **Viewing** activity on Activity Master 3, p. 60.

Post-viewing
Have students pretend they've procured a summer job as a tour guide for German tourists. Have them plan an itinerary for a local walking or bus tour and write a script for their tour. (If the local sights are not too compelling, students may want to write their tours for another location, either for a famous city [Chicago, New York, San Francisco] or for another city they've lived in.)

Landeskunde

Pre-viewing
Have everybody name his or her three favorite foods. Supply German vocabulary as necessary, or have students look up new words in a dictionary. Make a composite list of the class's favorite foods on the board.

Viewing
Have students write down the foods they hear mentioned. If something is repeated, have them make a tally mark next to that food.

Post-viewing
Compare the class list of favorite foods with the list of foods from the video. Are there similarities? Differences? What cultural conclusions can the students draw from the similarities and differences in their reponses?

Videoclips: Werbung

Pre-viewing
Tell students they are going to see several commercials for the German postal service. Have them list services you can expect when you go to a post office in the United States.

Viewing
See **Viewing** activity on Activity Master 3, p. 60.

Post-viewing
Based on what they learned from these commercials, have students discuss the differences between the German and the American postal systems.

Name _____ Klasse _____ Datum _____

Activity Master 1

Los geht's!

Viewing

1. If the sentences below are correct, check **stimmt**. If not, check **stimmt nicht**. If any sentence is incorrect, restate it correctly. Write the corrected statements in the blanks provided.

Supplementary Vocabulary	
gesund	healthy
Gern geschehen.	You're welcome.

	Stimmt	Stimmt nicht	
1. Mara und Markus trinken Cola.	_____	_____	(_____)
2. Die Touristen wollen zum Marienplatz gehen.	_____	_____	(_____)
3. Die Amerikaner kommen aus Minnesota.	_____	_____	(_____)
4. Markus und Mara essen Bratwurst.	_____	_____	(_____)
5. Die Amerikaner probieren den Leberkäs.	_____	_____	(_____)
6. Markus und Mara haben keine Zeit, den Amerikanern die Stadt zu zeigen.	_____	_____	(_____)

Post-viewing

2. Listen to the **Los geht's!** segment again, and write down any expressions you hear that give directions for getting somewhere.
   _____

3. Imagine that you are Mara or Markus and that you are eating at an **Imbissstube** in front of the subway station. A German-speaking tourist asks you for directions to the **Hofbräuhaus**. Using the map on p. 249 of your textbook, how will you tell him or her to get there?
   _____
   _____

Landeskunde (in *Pupil's Edition*)

Supplementary Vocabulary	
das Currywürstchen	a spicy sausage popular in Berlin

Pre-viewing

4. List as many German foods as you can think of. Have you tried any of them? From your list, circle the ones you've tried and put a star next to the ones you really like (or think you might really like).
   _____
   _____

Viewing

5. Based on the information they gave in their interviews, which of the people interviewed (Melina, Rosi, or Uli) might have made the following statements? Write the correct name in the blank in front of each statement.

   _____ 1. Ich mag Apfelstrudel.   _____ 3. Ich mag Obst sehr gern.

   _____ 2. Ich esse Weißwurst gern.

58 Video Guide   German 1 Komm mit!

Name _____ Klasse _____ Datum _____

Activity Master 2

Landeskunde (on Video only)

Supplementary Vocabulary			
Spätzle (pl)	noodles	der Fisch	fish
das Meer	the ocean	Knödel (pl)	dumplings
Speckknödel (pl)	bacon-flavored dumplings	rote Beete	beets
Rouladen mit Klößen	rolled meat with dumplings	deutsche Kost	German food
Kohlrouladen (pl)	rolled cabbage stuffed with meat	Mohrrüben (pl)	carrots

Pre-viewing

1. Ask three people in your class **Was isst du gern?** Record their names and their answers here.

   1. _____
   2. _____
   3. _____

2. Now compile a report based on your and your classmates' information to determine the most popular foods in the class.

Viewing

3. Below is a list of all the foods mentioned in the interviews. As you listen to the video again, keep a tally of the foods to find out which ones are mentioned most often as favorite foods.

   _____ Eis   _____ Schnitzel   _____ Linseneintopf
   _____ Gulasch   _____ Paprika   _____ Eierkuchen
   _____ Kaiserschmarren   _____ Pizza   _____ Gemüse
   _____ Hamburger   _____ Cheeseburger   _____ Tortellini
   _____ Ravioli   _____ Spätzle   _____ Pommes
   _____ Fisch   _____ rote Beete   _____ Knödel
   _____ Speckknödel   _____ Salat   _____ Spaghetti
   _____ Strudel   _____ Süßigkeiten   _____ Wurst
   _____ Lasagne   _____ Rouladen mit Klößen _____ Kohlrouladen

Post-viewing

4. Several nationalities are mentioned as the interviewees talk about their favorite foods from around the world. Circle the ones you recall from the video segment.

   österreichisch   amerikanisch   Schweizer   italienisch   deutsch
   chinesisch   asiatisch   spanisch   schottisch   mexikanisch
   ungarisch   griechisch   vietnamesisch   indonesisch   türkisch

5. Do the people interviewed mention foods that no one in your class mentioned in the **Pre-viewing** activity? What are they?

   _____

6. Did the people in your class mention foods that were not mentioned in the video? What are they?

   _____

7. Can you draw any conclusions about cultural influences in the United States and Germany, based on the foods that appear to be most popular in the two countries?

   _____

German 1 Komm mit!   Video Guide

Name _____ Klasse _____ Datum _____

Activity Master 3

Fortsetzung

> **Supplementary Vocabulary**
> der Strauss-Brunnen   the Strauss Fountain

Viewing

8. According to Mara, what are some of the activities that one can do at the **Marienplatz**? Circle the ones that she mentions and that you see portrayed in the video.

   Basketball spielen   einkaufen gehen   essen   ins Kino gehen
   lesen   miteinander sprechen   Musik hören   Obst kaufen
   schlafen   singen   trinken   auf Freunde warten

9. Match the sights in Munich with the statements Mara makes about each sight.

   _____ 1. das Münchner Kindl   a. Hier kann man Opern hören.
   _____ 2. der Dom   b. Da sieht man viele Radfahrer und Fußgänger.
   _____ 3. die Fußgängerzone   c. Es ist das Wahrzeichen der Stadt.
   _____ 4. das Nationaltheater   d. Hier fahren keine Autos.
   _____ 5. Schloss Nymphenburg   e. Er hat zwei Türme.
   _____ 6. das Deutsche Museum   f. Die Könige von Bayern haben hier gewohnt.
   _____ 7. der Englische Garten   g. Der ist der älteste Lebensmittelmarkt in München.
   _____ 8. der Viktualienmarkt   h. Man braucht viele Tage, um alles da zu sehen.

Videoclips: Werbung

Pre-viewing

10. List as many services as you can that one can get through the post office (in the United States).
    _____

Viewing

11. Place a check mark beside those activities that you saw portrayed in the video segment.

    _____ Auto fahren   _____ Boot fahren
    _____ mit dem Zug fahren   _____ Rad fahren
    _____ einen Computer benutzen   _____ mit Kindern spielen
    _____ Schach spielen

12. Was macht man bei „Nordsee"?
    a. Pizza essen   c. Fisch essen
    b. Obst und Gemüse kaufen   d. Schach und Karten spielen

Post-viewing

13. Was kann man auf der Post machen? _____

14. What appear to be some differences between the German and American postal systems?
    _____

60 Video Guide   German 1 Komm mit!

Location Opener for Chapters 10-12

Location: Baden-Württemberg

Start Time: 1:14
Length: 2:46
Student textbook pp. 272-275

The language in this location opener is authentic German spoken at a normal rate and may be difficult for students to understand. It should be made clear to them that they are not expected to understand everything. The types of activities you choose to do with them should be designed to help them understand the major points; the activities included for this section have been designed with this in mind. (script on p. 103)

Teaching Suggestions

Pre-viewing

1. Have students locate Baden-Württemberg on the map on p. 272 or on p. 2 of their textbooks. Have them tell you the names of the states that border it. Have them look at the photos on pp. 274-275 and tell you their impression of Baden-Württemberg.

2. Go through pp. 274-275 of the *Pupil's Edition* with the students. Use the information in the *Teacher's Edition* on pp. 271A-271B to provide background information about Bietigheim and Baden-Württemberg in general.

3. Before showing the Location Opener, ask students to watch it with the following questions in mind: What clues in the photos give them information about the type of city Bietigheim is and the kinds of events that take place there? Based on these impressions, what kind of city do they think Bietigheim is? Is it a large metropolis, or is it a smaller city? Is it old? Modern? Traditional? Have them explain their impressions.

Viewing

Step 1 Show the video once without sound and discuss with the class the answers to the above questions about Bietigheim. They may not have enough information to answer them yet, but they will get more information each time they view the segment.

Step 2 Show the video again without sound, having them write down the major attractions they see in the order they see them. (Let them use even simple answers at this point, such as *building* or *marketplace,* as long as they accurately convey what is in the video.)

Step 3 Help students work their way through the Supplementary Vocabulary on the Activity Master. Help students see that they can make intelligent guesses about meaning by looking for cognates.

Step 4 Show the video with sound, and have students complete the Location Opener activities on p. 62.

Post-viewing

1. Have students, working either in groups or with a partner, compare their answers on the Activity Master. Play the video once again, if necessary.

2. Make statements and have students say whether they are correct (**stimmt**) or incorrect (**stimmt nicht**), e.g.: **Der Schwarzwald ist in Baden-Württemberg. (stimmt)** or **Stuttgart ist die Landeshauptstadt von Baden-Württemberg. (stimmt)** Have them correct statements that are false.

3. Go back to the general questions about Bietigheim that you posed before viewing and discuss the answers. Have students defend their answers by referring to what they saw in the video. Lead students into a discussion of some cultural issues by asking the following questions:

    What kinds of traditions do you think a city like Bietigheim might have? How would they compare it with other cities they have learned about (Hamburg, Wedel, München)? Would Bietigheim possibly have more in common with Hamburg or with Wedel? Why?

Name _____ Klasse _____ Datum _____

Activity Master: Location Opener

Supplementary Vocabulary			
nordwestlich von	northwest of	mittelalterlich	medieval
das Stadttor	city gate	prachtvoll	magnificent
die Kirche	church		
von grünen Weinbergen umgeben	surrounded by green vineyards		
die Evangelische Stadtkirche	Protestant City Church		
die Burg	fortress	das Schloss	castle
das Fachwerkhaus	half-timbered building	die Hexe	witch
das Hexenwegle	Witches' Walk		

Viewing

1. Circle the word that completes the sentence according to what Sabine says.
   1. Bietigheim liegt *25 / 45* Kilometer nordwestlich von Stuttgart.
   2. Besigheim ist eine *mittelalterliche / sehr moderne* Stadt.
   3. Sabines Heimatstadt ist *Bietigheim / Stuttgart.*
   4. Die Hauptstraße in Bietigheim ist jetzt *ein Marktplatz / eine Fußgängerzone.*
   5. Das Kleine Bürgerhaus ist ein Fachwerkhaus aus dem *17. / 15.* Jahrhundert.
   6. Jeden *Freitag / Samstag* ist Markttag auf dem Rathausplatz.
   7. Das Hexenwegle ist eine lustige *Gasse / Gegend.*

2. Match the place with what Mara says about it.

   _____ 1. Besigheim   a. ein Fachwerkhaus aus dem 17. Jahrhundert

   _____ 2. die Stadtkirche   b. erbaut in den Jahren 1401 bis 1411

   _____ 3. das Rathaus   c. eine kleine mittelalterliche Stadt

   _____ 4. das Bürgerhaus   d. ein prachtvoller Bau

Post-viewing

3. What parts of the city of Bietigheim would you most like to visit? Write a short paragraph describing the place or places, basing your description on anything you saw in the video or in your textbook, as well as information you have heard or read.

_____
_____
_____
_____
_____
_____
_____
_____
_____

KAPITEL 10 — Kino und Konzerte

Functions modeled in video:
- expressing likes and dislikes
- expressing familiarity
- expressing preferences and favorites
- talking about what you did in your free time

Video Segment	Correlation to Print Materials — Pupil's Edition	Video Guide — Activity Masters	Video Guide — Scripts	Videocassette 4 — Start Time	Videocassette 4 — Length	Videocassette 5 (captioned) — Start Time	Videocassette 5 (captioned) — Length
Los geht's!	pp. 278–279	p. 66	p. 103	4:02	4:05	55:12	4:04
Fortsetzung		pp. 67–68	pp. 103–104	8:10	3:05	59:19	3:06
Landeskunde	p. 289*	pp. 66, 67	pp. 104–105	11:53	3:30		
Videoclips		p. 68	p. 105	15:35	4:08		

*The *Video Program* provides film footage of the Landeskunde interviews in the *Pupil's Edition* and additional interviews.

Video Synopses

Los geht's! *Wie verbringt ihr eure Freizeit?*

A couple walks through a garden chatting amiably about the lovely flowers. The man sees a group of teenagers lounging in the garden and suggests that young people today are lazy and sit around doing nothing. The teenagers object and break into song, showing that they don't just sit around but have plenty of things to do, ranging from helping older people to skateboarding.

Andreas and Nicole are at the box office of a movie theater, waiting for Sabine, Sandra, and Martin. When Nicole says that Sabine is probably at home reading, the camera cuts to Sabine, at home, who explains how she loves to read and has many books. As Andreas says that Sandra and Martin have probably stopped to look at music cassettes, the camera cuts to Sandra and Martin, who are indeed in a record store, comparing tastes in music. Thomas comes along to the theater, listening to music on his portable cassette player. Finally Sabine, Martin, and Sandra arrive. All of them discuss which film they want to see, the action film or the fantasy film. Although Nicole expresses her dislike for action films, that is the film they decide to see.

Fortsetzung

After the film, the teenagers exchange opinions about it, agreeing in general that they didn't enjoy it very much. They go to watch a video. A music video by *Die Prinzen* closes the segment.

Landeskunde

Students of various ages from different locations talk about the cultural events they attend.

Videoclips: Werbung

1. *Die unendliche Geschichte:* video
2. *Gute Zeiten/Schlechte Zeiten:* music CD
3. Andreas Elsholz: CD-single
4. Howard Carpendale: album
5. *Bravo Hits 4:* album
6. NDR 2 Open Air Festival: concert
7. Leibnitz Butterkeks: cookies
8. *Rätselhafte Phänomene:* magazine

German 1 Komm mit!

Teaching Suggestions

Captioned Video
Both **Los geht's!** and **Fortsetzung** are available with German captions on Videocassette 5.

Los geht's!

Pre-viewing
Ask students what they like to do with friends on a lazy afternoon. Have them interview each other and then report their findings back to the class, or to a small group.

Viewing
See **Viewing** activity on Activity Master 1, p. 66

Post-viewing
Have students use the list on the Activity Master 1 on p. 66 to indicate the types of things they like to do with their friends. Have them rank the activities they've indicated according to how much time they spend doing them. Conduct a class survey to see which activity the class as a whole spends the most time doing.

Fortsetzung

Pre-viewing
Have students look at the movie ads on pp. 294-295 in their books and categorize each movie according to its genre. Have them interview each other, asking **Welchen Film siehst du lieber?**, and **Hast du „Groundhog Day" schon gesehen?** Have them report their findings to the rest of the class.

Viewing
Have students think of films they know of that the teenagers might be seeing. That is, have them name some popular fantasy and action films.

Post-viewing
Take a class survey of film likes and dislikes. Ask **Wer mag Horrorfilme?** and have students raise their hands, to find out the class's favorite and least favorite kinds of films. Have them name films of those genres.

Landeskunde

Pre-viewing
Ask students to list all cultural events they can think of in German. Supply additional vocabulary as necessary, or have them look terms up in the dictionary. Then take a class survey by naming each event and having students raise their hands if they go to or would like to go to such an event.

Viewing
Have students use the list made during the **Pre-viewing** activity to keep a tally of the events mentioned by the people interviewed.

Post-viewing
Compare the class survey with the survey of people in the video. Is there a considerable difference? Why might that be?

Videoclips: Werbung

Pre-viewing
Take a survey: If students were given the option to go to a rock-concert, an opera, a symphony concert, the museum of their choice, the ballet, the movie of their choice, or to buy some CDs and stay home and listen to them, which would they choose?

Viewing
Play the commercials once without sound and have students identify what they are advertising. Then play them again with sound and have them verify their hypotheses. Play them once more and have them do the **Viewing** activity on Activity Master 3, p. 68.

Post-viewing
Have students try to categorize the films they saw advertised as **Komödie, Horrorfilm, Abenteuerfilm,** etc. Ask them which of the rock groups they have heard of.

Name _____ Klasse _____ Datum _____

Activity Master 1

KAPITEL 10

Los geht's!

Supplementary Vocabulary			
warten	to wait	kegeln	to bowl
segeln	to sail	traurig	sad
der Faulenzer	someone who is lazy	abholen	to pick up (someone)
die „Toten Hosen"	a popular German rock band		

Viewing

1. Circle the activities mentioned by the teenagers.

alten Leuten helfen	in die Oper gehen	kochen	schreiben
basteln	ins Theater gehen	lachen	segeln
diskutieren	ins Kino gehen	lesen	singen
Fernsehen schauen	joggen	musizieren	Skateboard fahren
Fußball spielen	Karten spielen	radeln	traurig sein
Hausaufgaben machen	kegeln	Schach spielen	warten

Post-viewing

2. First match the action with the person doing that action, and then express as a complete sentence what that person or those people are doing.

   1. Martin   5. Nicole   a. warten
   2. Sandra   6. Sabine   b. lesen
   3. Thomas   c. Kassetten anschauen
   4. Andreas   d. die „Toten Hosen" anhören

3. Was sehen die Freunde?   a. einen Fantasyfilm   b. einen Actionfilm

Landeskunde (in *Pupil's Edition*)

Supplementary Vocabulary			
kulturelle Veranstaltungen	cultural performances/events	das Ballett	ballet
die Karte	ticket	die Vergünstigung	discount
witzig	funny	die Ausstellung	exhibit
günstig	here: reasonably priced	Schwanensee	Swan Lake

Viewing

4. Match each sentence with the student most likely to have said it.

   Silvana   Silke   Tim   Rosi

   _____ 1. Ich gehe Freitagabend ins Theater, um *Romeo und Julia* zu sehen. Dann am Samstag gehe ich in eine Austellung von Paul Klee.

   _____ 2. Meine Eltern haben mich in die Oper eingeladen, aber ich will nicht mitgehen, weil ich mich am Samstag mit Freunden treffe.

   _____ 3. Meine Mutter und ich haben Karten fürs Ballett *Peter und der Wolf* von Prokofjew für nächste Woche.

   _____ 4. Ich möchte gern *Die Zauberflöte* von Mozart sehen, aber die Karten sind teuer, und ich bekomme keine Vergünstigung über die Schule.

Name _____ Klasse _____ Datum _____

Activity Master 2

KAPITEL 10

Landeskunde (on Video only)

Supplementary Vocabulary		
draußen aufgeführt werden	*to be played (shown) outside*	die Auswahl *selection, choice*
ausverkauft	*sold out*	momentan *at the moment*

Viewing

1. Keep a tally of the types of cultural events these people like to attend.

   _____ Opern

   _____ Kinos

   _____ Theateraufführungen

   _____ Konzerte

   _____ Ballette

   _____ Ausstellungen

   _____ Museen

Post-viewing

2. Circle the two events listed above that you attend most often or would most like to attend. Are your favorite events ones that appear to be popular with the Germans interviewed? Which of the two events listed above are the most popular in your class? Does this seem similar to or different from the preferences of the Germans? How can you explain this similarity or difference?

   _____

   _____

Fortsetzung

Viewing

3. Fill in the missing words.

   > krank ehrlich Bank Millionär
   > Geld Freund Freundin Konto

   Ich wär so gerne Millionär

   Dann wär' mein Konto niemals leer.

   Ich wär so gerne Millionär, millionenschwer!

   Ich hab kein 1 _____, hab keine Ahnung, doch ich hab ein großes Maul. Weder

   Doktor noch Professor, aber ich bin stinkfaul. Ich habe keine reiche

   2 _____ und keinen reichen 3 _____.

   Von viel Kohle hab ich bisher leider nur geträumt. Was soll ich tun, was soll

German 1 Komm mit!   Video Guide **67**

Activity Master 3

ich machen? Bin vor Kummer schon halb 4 _____. Hab mir schon 'n paar Mal überlegt, vielleicht knackst du eine 5 _____. Doch das ist leider sehr gefährlich, bestimmt werd ich gefasst. Und außerdem bin ich doch 6 _____, und will nicht in den Knast.

Ich wär so gerne 7 _____. Dann wär' mein 8 _____ niemals leer. Ich wär so gerne Millionär, millionenschwer! Ich wär so gerne Millionär.

Videoclips: Werbung

Supplementary Vocabulary

die Zeitschrift	magazine/periodical	Gute Zeiten, Schlechte Zeiten	Good Times, Bad Times
das Original-Autogramm	original autograph	fertig geworden	here: ready, finished
die Eintrittskarte	admission ticket	die Vorverkaufsstelle	advance ticket location
die Tageskasse	box office	die Erklärung	explanation
rätselhafte Phänomene	mysterious phenomena	das Geheimnis	secret

Viewing

4. If someone were to treat you to two of the things or events advertised, which would you pick? Watch the commercials, then indicate which two things or events you would like to be treated to.

   Die unendliche Geschichte   Super Hits—Die Toten Hosen, etc.
   Das Geisterhaus   Music Festival
   Andreas Elsholz' neue CD   Ein Abend in der Oper
   CD: Ganz Nah—Howard Carpendale   Rätselhafte Phänomene

Post-viewing

5. Was ist dein/deine

   Lieblingsfilm? _____

   Lieblingsmusik? _____

   Lieblings-CD oder -Kassette? _____

   Lieblingsbuch? _____

   Lieblingsstar? _____

   Lieblingszeitschrift? _____

6. You are a reporter doing on-the-street interviews for your cultural interest column. Get together with two other people and interview them about their favorite books, films, music, etc. Be prepared to answer their questions, because they are also reporters doing the same interviews for their newspapers.

KAPITEL 11 — Der Geburtstag

Functions modeled in video:
- using the telephone in Germany
- inviting someone to a party and accepting or declining
- talking about birthdays and expressing good wishes
- discussing gift ideas

Video Segment	Pupil's Edition	Video Guide — Activity Masters	Video Guide — Scripts	Videocassette 4 — Start Time	Videocassette 4 — Length	Videocassette 5 (captioned) — Start Time	Videocassette 5 (captioned) — Length
Los geht's!	pp. 306-307	p. 72	pp. 105-106	19:53	2:15	1:02:31	1:41
Fortsetzung		p. 73	p. 106	22:12	1:20	1:04:45	0:52
Landeskunde	p. 316*	pp. 72, 73	pp. 106-107	23:38	4:19		
Videoclips		p. 74	p. 107	27:12	2:36		

*The *Video Program* provides film footage of the Landeskunde interviews in the *Pupil's Edition* and additional interviews.

Video Synopses

Los geht's! *Geschenke aussuchen*

In this segment of the video, Nicole calls Sabine to invite her to the birthday party she is organizing for Martin. Later, Sabine and Nicole go shopping and discuss what they should give Martin for his birthday. Finally, Nicole decides to get him a T-shirt and also finds a birthday card that she likes.

Fortsetzung

Sabine and Nicole talk about Thomas' birthday. When Nicole looks it up in her calendar, she discovers that Martin's birthday is not next Saturday, but rather in August! She doesn't know what to do, because she has already planned the party for him for Saturday!

Landeskunde

People of various ages from different cities talk about what they give friends and relatives for their birthdays.

Videoclips: Werbung

1. **Milka:** chocolates
2. **Merci:** chocolates
3. **Brockhaus:** encyclopedias

Teaching Suggestions

Captioned Video
Both **Los geht's!** and **Fortsetzung** are available with German captions on Videocassette 5.

Los geht's!

Pre-viewing
Have students brainstorm vocabulary about gifts by asking them questions such as: **Was schenkst du deiner Mutter (deinem Vater, Bruder) zum Geburtstag?** Write the relevant vocabulary on the board, and encourage students to look up new vocabulary in their dictionaries.

Viewing
See **Viewing** activity on Activity Master 1, p. 72.

Post-viewing
Have students discuss the people in their lives for whom it is easy to buy gifts, and the people for whom it is difficult to buy gifts. In those difficult situations, what do the students do to come up with gift ideas?

Fortsetzung

Pre-viewing
Collect all the birth dates in the classroom. Find out during which season most of your students were born. Who has birthdays during summer vacation? Do those students celebrate their birthdays with their friends, or are their friends usually gone? If so, what do they do to celebrate their birthdays?

Viewing
See **Viewing** activity on Activity Master 2, p. 73.

Post-viewing
Ask what the conflict is (Martin's birthday is on August 18, but Nicole is having a party for him on Saturday, because she thought Saturday was his birthday). What would your students do in the same situation? Call off the party? Take back the presents? Find someone else whose birthday is coming up to be the guest of honor?

Landeskunde

Pre-viewing
Have students get together in groups and discuss what they would give the following people as gifts: each other, the teacher, their best friend, their younger brother or sister, another younger child, their parents, their grandparents or another older person.

Viewing
See **Viewing** activity on Activity Master 2, p. 73.

Post-viewing
Ask students to write down a birthday-wish list in German. Collect the lists (without names on them) and hand them back out randomly. Have students find the person who wrote the list they received by asking several students questions such as **Was möchtest du zum Geburtstag? Möchtest du (eine CD)?** Or have them pretend they are going to give the things on the list: **Ich schenke jemandem eine Armbanduhr. Möchtest du eine?**

Videoclips: Werbung

Pre-viewing
Have students brainstorm a list of inexpensive gifts they can give people they don't know very well. Have them brainstorm a list of more elaborate gifts that would be given by people who know each other very well.

Viewing
See **Viewing** activity on Activity Master 3, p. 74.

Post-viewing
Have students write sentences using the gift ideas from the commercials, saying to whom they would give each gift.

Example: **Meinem Bruder schenke ich Milka Schokolade.**

Name _____ Klasse _____ Datum _____

Activity Master 1

Los geht's!

Supplementary Vocabulary			
der Komponist	*composer*	eine Karte	*card*

Viewing

1. Indicate whether the following sentences are **a)** correct or **b)** incorrect, according to the video. Fill in the correct information for incorrect sentences.

    1. _____ Sandra (_____) hat am Samstag Geburtstag.
    2. _____ Nicole kauft eine CD (_____) als Geschenk.
    3. _____ Martin hat noch keinen CD-Spieler (_____).
    4. _____ Sabine kauft ein Buch (_____) als Geschenk.

Post-viewing

2. Imagine the following people are having birthdays. What would you give them?

    dem Deutschlehrer/ der Deutschlehrerin _____

    deinem besten Freund/deiner besten Freundin _____

    deinem Bruder/deiner Schwester _____

    deiner Oma/deinem Opa _____

Landeskunde (in *Pupil's Edition*)

Supplementary Vocabulary			
s. unterhalten	*converse*	Ähnliches	*something similar*
die Kleinigkeit	*little thing/trifle*	der Gutschein	*gift certificate*
etwas Selbstgemachtes	*something handmade*	ein bemaltes T-Shirt	*a painted T-shirt*

Post-viewing

3. Who would say what? Next to each person's name, write the letter of the thing he or she is most likely to say.

    _____ 1. Eva
    _____ 2. Jutta
    _____ 3. Melanie
    _____ 4. Rosi

    a. Ich gehe heute auf eine Fete zu einem Mädchen, das ich nicht so gut kenne. Ich schenke ihr eine Kaffeetasse.

    b. Ich gehe heute auf eine Fete zu meiner besten Freundin, aber wie immer weiß ich nicht, was ich schenken soll. Tja, ich schenke ihr halt einen Gutschein für eine CD.

    c. Meine Freundin Silke hat heute Geburtstag. Ich schenke ihr dieses schöne selbst bemalte T-Shirt.

    d. Mein Freund Max hat am Samstag Geburtstag. Ich habe für ihn eine Fete organisiert. Ich habe Max und ein paar Freunde zu mir eingeladen. Wir werden essen, uns schön unterhalten und Musik hören.

KAPITEL 11

Name _____ Klasse _____ Datum _____

Activity Master 2

Landeskunde (on Video only)

Supplementary Vocabulary			
die Flasche Sekt	*bottle of champagne*	mieten	*to rent*
ausgefallen	*strange, weird*	ausgeflippt	*flipped out*
witzig	*funny*		

Viewing

1. Circle the items you hear mentioned as gifts.

   Armbanduhr   Bild   Blumen
   Bücher   CDs   Gutscheine
   Kalender   Kassetten Kleinigkeiten
   Lego™   Parfüm   Poster
   Pralinen   Schmuck   T-Shirt

Post-viewing

2. Go back and underline the gifts that you like to give people for their birthdays. Now interview another person in your class. In German, ask what he or she gives people for their birthdays. Keep track of your partner's answers by putting a check mark next to the items he or she mentions. Switch roles and answer the same question for your partner.

Fortsetzung

Supplementary Vocabulary			
irgendwann	*sometime*	die Ferien	*vacation*

Viewing

3. Circle the word that completes the sentence correctly according to what you saw in the video.
   1. Thomas hat Geburtstag irgendwann im *Frühling/Sommer/Winter/Herbst.*
   2. Sein Geburtstag ist im *Mai/Januar/Oktober/August.*
   3. Seinen Geburtstag feiern sie *oft/nie/jedes Jahr/am Samstag.*
   4. Thomas' Geburtstag ist am *ersten Mai/elften August/zwölften Oktober/dritten Januar.*
   5. Martin hat am *Samstag/achtzehnten August/ersten Mai/elften August* Geburtstag.

Post-viewing

4. What is the problem with Martin's birthday party?

   _____
   _____

German 1 Komm mit!   Video Guide 73

Name _____ Klasse _____ Datum _____

Activity Master 3

Videoclips: Werbung

Supplementary Vocabulary

der Weihnachtsmann	Santa Claus	der Farbenklecks	flecks of color
die Versuchung	temptation	die Wasserflut	flood
der Sonnenstrahl	sunshine/ray of sunlight	der Fels	cliff
der Wüstensand	desert sand	zum Nulltarif	without tariff/free
die Brandung	surf, breakers	Langeweile haben	to be bored
die Nuss	nut		

Viewing

5. Write in the letter of the person (people) to whom you think it would be most appropriate to give the items advertised as gifts.

   _____ 1. Milka Schokolade

   _____ 2. Merci Schokolade

   _____ 3. Brockhaus Enzyklopädie und Geschenke

   a. a young child
   b. boyfriend or girlfriend
   c. mother/father
   d. older relative (great aunt/uncle, grandparent)
   e. teacher
   f. husband/wife
   g. best friend
   h. student

Post-viewing

6. Which of the above would you most like to have for your birthday?
   _____

7. Which would you like to give to your best friend?
   _____

8. Which would you give to your grandparents (or other older friends/relatives)?
   _____

KAPITEL 11

KAPITEL 12 Die Fete

Functions modeled in video:
- offering help and explaining what to do
- asking where something is located and giving directions
- making plans and inviting someone to come along
- talking about clothing
- discussing gift ideas
- describing people and places
- saying what you would like and whether you do or don't want more
- talking about what you did

Video Segment	Correlation to Print Materials			Videocassette 4		Videocassette 5 (captioned)	
	Pupil's Edition	Video Guide		Start Time	Length	Start Time	Length
		Activity Masters	Scripts				
Los geht's!	pp. 334-335	p. 78	pp. 107-108	31:05	4:48	1:05:44	4:48
Fortsetzung		p. 79	pp. 108-109	35:58	4:17	1:10:36	4:18
Landeskunde	p. 341*	pp. 78, 79	pp. 109-110	40:55	4:20		
Videoclips		p. 80	p. 110	45:30	4:00		

*The *Video Program* provides film footage of the Landeskunde interviews in the *Pupil's Edition* and additional interviews.

Video Synopses

Los geht's! *Die Geburtstagsfete*

In this segment of the video, Nicole and her friends prepare for a party to celebrate Martin's birthday.

Fortsetzung

The segment continues as guests arrive for the party bearing birthday gifts for Martin. After everyone has something to drink and eat, they sing "Happy Birthday" to Martin.

Landeskunde

People of various ages from different cities talk about how they help out at home.

Videoclips: Werbung

1. **Konditorei Coppenrath u. Wiese:** frozen cakes
2. **Konditorei Coppenrath u. Wiese:** frozen cakes
3. **Tengelmann und Kaisers:** vegetables
4. **Frosta:** frozen dinners
5. **Neudorff Bio-Fibel:** environmental products

German 1 Komm mit!   Video Guide

Teaching Suggestions

Captioned Video
Both **Los geht's!** and **Fortsetzung** are available with German captions on Videocassette 5.

Los geht's!

Pre-viewing
Have students get together in groups of three or four to plan a birthday party for another student. One student should act as secretary and record all the decisions. Have them decide when and where the party will be and whom they will invite. They should also decide what tasks need to be done and distribute the tasks among themselves. Finally, have them make a grocery list and discuss gift ideas.

Viewing
Each student will need a copy of the list of things they decided need to be done for their party. Have students circle the tasks on their lists that are done in the video and write down who in the video did them. If there are tasks done in the video that are not on their lists, have them record those and who did them, as well.

Post-viewing
Have students get together in groups of two or three. Each group should make a list of the ingredients necessary for making a cake. They can role-play asking where those ingredients are at a grocery store and then buying them. Then the group should determine the steps involved in baking a cake.

Fortsetzung

Pre-viewing
Review dative expressions with and without pronouns, and review the conversational past with **geben** and **schenken**. Have students ask each other questions such as **Was hast du deiner Mutter zum Geburtstag gegeben/geschenkt? Ich habe ihr eine Armbanduhr geschenkt.** They should ask about a variety of friends and relatives.

Viewing
See **Viewing** activity on Activity Master 2, p. 79.

Post-viewing
Have students plan a real party to be held during the last class session, or sometime outside of class. Have them decide what kind of music, food, and cake to have. Suggest that everybody bring a small gift (something they have at home or something that costs less than $3.00), wrapped, with no name on it, and that they have an anonymous gift exchange.

Landeskunde

Pre-viewing
Take a class survey of things students have to do at home to help out. Encourage students to paraphrase or describe chores for which they don't have the appropriate vocabulary, rather than using the English word.

Viewing
See **Viewing** activity on Activity Master 1, p. 78.

Post-viewing
In pairs, have students act out situations in which the parent is asking the child to do some household chores, but the student has other plans. Have them work out a compromise. One student plays the parent and the other plays the child. Then have them switch roles.

Videoclips: Werbung

Pre-viewing
Ask students if they would rather bake or buy a cake for a party they were hosting. Have them brainstorm vocabulary of things you can cook on a grill outdoors. Ask if anyone keeps a compost heap at their home, and how they maintain it.

Viewing
See **Viewing** activity on Activity Master 3, p. 80.

Post-viewing
Ask students who prepares the meals in their household. Ask whether they ever use frozen dinners such as **Frosta**.

Name _____ Klasse _____ Datum _____

Activity Master 1

Los geht's!

Supplementary Vocabulary			
genügend	enough	die Portion	portion
rühren	to stir	das Backpulver	baking powder
vergessen	to forget	die Mülltonne	garbage can
kompostieren	to compost	der Komposthaufen	compost heap
umweltfreundlich	environmentally aware	pünktlich	punctual
Lieb von dir!	That's nice of you!	fleißig	hard-working

Viewing

1. Everybody is helping Nicole prepare for the party. But who is doing what? Next to each person's name, write the letter of the task he or she is doing to help.

   _____ 1. Nicole   a. Gemüse waschen
   _____ 2. Thomas   b. einkaufen gehen
   _____ 3. Nicole's father   c. den Rasen mähen
   _____ 4. Andreas   d. den Kuchen backen
                                 e. den Müll sortieren und wegbringen

Post-viewing

2. If you were having a party, who would help you prepare for it?
   _____
   _____

3. What would you have to do to prepare for a party? Make a list of tasks, and say who would do each task.   Example: einkaufen gehen.   Meine Mutter geht für mich einkaufen.
   _____
   _____
   _____
   _____

Landeskunde (in *Pupil's Edition*)

Viewing

4. Write the letter of each task beside the name of the person who mentions doing that task. Remember, each person may mention more than one task, and each task may be done by more than one person.

   1. Heide _____   a. Mülleimer runterbringen, den Müll rausbringen
   2. Silvana _____   b. Wäsche aufhängen
                                c. Staub saugen
   3. Monika _____   d. den Geschirrspüler ausräumen
                                e. den Rasen mähen
   4. Gerd _____   f. die Küche wischen
                                g. abwaschen
                                h. Toilette sauber machen
                                i. Zimmer aufräumen

KAPITEL 12

Name _____ Klasse _____ Datum _____

Activity Master 2

Landeskunde (on Video only)

Supplementary Vocabulary			
bügeln	to iron	erwarten	to expect
nerven	to get on one's nerves		
Meine Oma ist vor kurzem gestorben.		My grandmother died recently.	

Viewing

1. Keep a tally of the household jobs the students mention.

   _____ abwaschen   _____ den Rasen mähen
   _____ den Müll rausbringen   _____ den Geschirrspüler ausräumen
   _____ die Küche wischen   _____ Fenster putzen
   _____ Mülleimer runterbringen _____ Staub saugen
   _____ Staub wischen   _____ Toilette sauber machen
   _____ Wäsche aufhängen   _____ Zimmer aufräumen

Post-viewing

2. Circle the jobs above that you do at home. Now interview another student and find out what he or she does at home. Put an X next to the jobs he or she mentions. Report your findings to the class.

Fortsetzung

Supplementary Vocabulary			
die Schürze	apron	die Bowle	punch
die Erdbeerbowle	strawberry punch	die Kerzen ausblasen	to blow out the candles

Viewing

3. Circle the foods and drinks you see or hear mentioned.

Getränke

Apfelsaft   Orangensaft
Cappuccino   Tee
Cola   Zitronenbowle
Erdbeerbowle
Fanta
Kaffee
Limo
Milch
Mineralwasser

Speisen

Aufschnitt   Krautsalat
Brezeln   Kuchen
Brot   Pommes
Gurkensalat   Schnitzel
Hackfleisch   Semmeln
Joghurt   Tomatensalat
Kaiserschmarren Wurstbrote
Karotten   Würstchen
Kartoffelsalat

Post-viewing

4. Invent a recipe for a **Bowle**. What will you call it? What are the ingredients?

   Meine Bowle heißt: _____

   Die Zutaten sind: _____

   _____

German 1 Komm mit!   Video Guide

Name _____ Klasse _____ Datum _____

Activity Master 3

Videoclips: Werbung

Supplementary Vocabulary			
tiefgekühlt	frozen	das Kotelett	cutlet
die Aubergine	eggplant	Austernpilze	oyster mushrooms
der Mais	corn	die Soße	sauce, gravy
mager	lean, nonfat	die Kräuter (pl)	herbs
das Gewürz	spice	die Mahlzeit	meal
naturgemäß gärtnern	to garden organically	kompostieren	to compost
Rasenschnitt	grass clippings		

Viewing

5. Match the name with the product:
   1. Konditorei Coppenrath u. Wiese (1)   a. Kompostier-System
   2. Konditorei Coppenrath u. Wiese (2)   b. Tiefgefrorene Torten
   3. Tengelmann u. Kaisers   c. Tiefgefrorenes Essen
   4. Frosta   d. Torten
   5. Neudorff Bio Fibel   e. Gemüse zum Grillen

Post-viewing

6. Isst du oft vom Grill? Wie oft?
   _____
   _____
   _____

7. Hast du schon mal gegrilltes Gemüse probiert?
   _____
   _____
   _____

8. Hast du schon mal gegrilles Obst probiert?
   _____
   _____
   _____

KAPITEL 12

80 Video Guide   German 1 Komm mit!

Video Scripts

LOCATION OPENER: Brandenburg

Hallo! Willkommen in Brandenburg, in der Hauptstadt Potsdam!

Ich heiße Jens Hartmann. Ich bin sechzehn und gehe auf das Helmholtz-Gymnasium. Potsdam ist eine historische Stadt und tausend Jahre alt. Hier in Potsdam gibt es viel zu sehen. Also, kommt mit, ich zeige euch meine Heimatstadt Potsdam.

Die Glienicker Brücke verbindet Berlin mit Potsdam. Diese Brücke war von 1945 bis 1989 gesperrt. Sie war der Ort, an dem die Spione von Ost und West ausgetauscht wurden.

Der alte Markt in Potsdam. Links die Nikolaikirche, 1724 als Barockkirche umgebaut, rechts das Alte Rathaus.

Unsere Fußgängerzone. Vor uns das Brandenburger Tor in Potsdam, das zur Zeit renoviert wird.

Ein sehenswertes Stadtviertel ist das Holländische Viertel, im holländischen Baustil 1733-42 errichtet, um holländische Einwanderer anzusiedeln.

Unsere größte Attraktion ist der Park Sanssouci, und das bekannteste Gebäude, Schloss Sanssouci. Hundertzweiunddreißig Stufen führen über den Weinberg hinauf zur Terrasse. Friedrich II., der Alte Fritz, begann mit diesem Projekt im Jahr 1744, vier Jahre nach seinem Regierungsantritt als König von Preußen.

Eine Marmorstatue Friedrichs des Großen.

Die sogenannten Neuen Kammern mit der wiedererrichteten Windmühle im Hintergrund.

Das Chinesische Teehaus. Lebensgroße vergoldete Teetrinker- und Musikantenfiguren schmücken diesen Rokokopavillon. Hier bat Friedrich der Große gelegentlich zum Tee.

Das Babelsberger Schloss ist aus den Jahren 1833-35. Es wurde von Karl Friedrich Schinkel erbaut. Als Vorbild diente Windsor Castle in England.

Schloss Cecilienhof, der letzte Schlossbau der Hohenzollern. Dieser Bau wurde 1913-17 für den Kronprinzen Wilhelm errichtet, im Stil eines englischen Landhauses. Dieses Schloss ist sehr bekannt. Hier unterschrieben im Jahre 1945 Churchill, Truman und Stalin das Potsdamer Abkommen.

Hier bin ich wieder, diesmal mit meinen Freunden. Wir möchten euch mehr von uns zeigen. Also, bis dann und tschüs!

KAPITEL 1
Wer bist du?

Los geht's!

– Hallo, Jens.
– Hallo!
– Ist das dein Moped?
– Ja.
– Super! Klasse!
– Ich komm jetzt immer mit dem Moped zur Schule.
– Ach ja! Du bist jetzt sechzehn!
– Hier!
– Oh, danke!
– Wer bist du denn? Bist du neu hier?
– Ja, ja ich bin neu hier.
– Und wie heißt du?
– Ich heiße Holger.
– Ich bin Jens, das ist Tara.
– Morgen, Tara!
– Guten Morgen, Holger. Woher kommst du denn?
– Aus Walburg.
– Walburg? Walburg? Wo liegt denn Walburg?
– In Hessen.
– Guten Morgen, Frau Weigel!
– Guten Morgen!
– Das ist Frau Weigel, unsere Biologielehrerin.
– Ach so!
– Schau mal, da kommt ja Ahmet! Hallo, Ahmet.
– Hallo, Tara, hallo, Jens. Was gibt's?
– Sag mal, Ahmet, ist morgen Training?
– Ja klar! Um drei Uhr.
– Ich bin Holger. Wie heißt du?
– Ahmet, Ahmet Özkan.
– Wie bitte? Öz...?

Kapitel 1 *cont.*

– Ich buchstabier's für dich: Ö- Z- K-A-N. Stimmt doch, oder?
– Ja, das stimmt.
– Und woher bist du?
– Aus der Türkei.
– Er ist der beste Mann bei uns im Team, die Nummer Eins!
– Ja prima!
– Schon gut, tschüs!
– Tschüs!

Fortsetzung

– Hallo, Ruhe bitte! Ruhe! Guten Morgen!
– Morgen!
– Ja, mein Name ist Gärtner, ich bin euer neuer Deutschlehrer.
– Schau, auch ein Neuer!
– Ja, ich sehe hier fünf Mädchen, sechs Jungen. Jetzt möchte ich natürlich auch wissen, wer ihr seid. Fangen wir doch am besten hier an. Wer bist du?
– Ich heiße Steffi Schilling.
– Und du, wer bist du?
– Ich bin Tara.
– Nur Tara? Dein Nachname, bitte!
– Tehrani.
– Ah, ja. Und du, junger Mann, wer bist du?
– Holger Warnecke.
– Bist du von hier?
– Nein, ich komme aus Walburg.
– Und du, wer bist du?
– Mein Name ist Ahmet Özkan. Ich bin aus der Türkei.
– Aus der Türkei. Ja, von wo da?
– Samsun, eine kleine Stadt am Schwarzen Meer.
– Ah ja, hier.
– Ahmet, sag mal, was heißt denn „Guten Tag" auf Türkisch?
– Mehrhaba.
– Kannst du uns kurz noch mal sagen, was „tschüs" auf Türkisch heißt?
– Güle Güle.
– Okay dann, „Güle Güle"! Na ja, tschüs und tschau bis morgen.

Landeskunde (in *Pupil's Edition*)

In Germany, many people of all ages ride bicycles—to school, to work, even to do their shopping. Why do you think this might be so? We asked many students how they get to school:

Wie kommst du zur Schule?

[Christina] Ich heiß Christina, bin 17 Jahre alt und komme mit dem Leichtkraftrad zur Schule.

[Sonja] Ich heiße Sonja Wegener. Ich bin 17 Jahre alt. Ich fahre meistens mit der U-Bahn zur Schule, aber im Sommer fahr ich auch mit Fahrrad.

[Sandra] Also, ich heiße Sandra Krabbel und ich bin 18 Jahre alt und meistens also, ich geh auf die Max-Beckmann-Oberschule und meistens fahre ich mit dem Bus. Aber ja, manchmal, ganz selten auch mit dem Fahrrad, und jetzt neuerdings auch manchmal mit dem Auto, aber nur sehr selten.

[Johannes] Also, ich heiße Johannes Hennicke, bin zwölf Jahre alt und fahre jeden Morgen mit dem Fahrrad zur Schule.

[Tim] Mein Name ist Tim Wiesbach. Ich bin 18 Jahre alt und komme mit meinem Moped jeden Tag, wenn das Wetter mitspielt, zur Schule.

Landeskunde (on Video only)

[Rosi] Ich heiße Rosi Kleinschmitt, bin 18 Jahre alt und geh auf die Max-Beckmann-Oberschule. Im Sommer komm ich meistens mit dem Fahrrad zur Schule und im Winter mit dem Bus.

[Jasmin] Also, ich heiße Jasmin Rosenkranz, wohne in Spandau und fahre mit dem Bus zur Schule. Dauert ungefähr 'ne Viertelstunde.

[Melanie] Ich heiße Melanie, Melanie Blützner und ich bin 16 Jahre alt. Ich werde nächsten Monat 17 Jahre. Und zur Schule fahre ich meistens mit dem Fahrrad, und wenn's gerade kaputt ist, dann geh ich meistens zu Fuß.

[Katja] Ich heiße Katja Schranowick, bin auch 16 und gehe zu Fuß zur Schule, weil sich das nicht lohnt, mit dem Fahrrad zu fahren, oder eben mit dem Bus.

[Björn] Ich heiße Björn. Ich bin 16 Jahre alt. Ich wohne hier gleich in der Nähe, und ich geh zu Fuß in die Schule—dauert nur ein paar Minuten.

Kapitel 1 *cont.*

[Ute] Ich heiße Ute, bin 17 Jahre alt und komme zu Fuß zur Schule.

[Helmut] Also, ich heiß Helmut, bin 12 Jahre alt und komme im Bus zur Schule.

[Maren] Also, ich heiß Maren Kreling, bin 12 Jahre alt und komme mit dem Fahrrad zur Schule.

[Johanna] Mit der U-Bahn.

[Jenny] Mit dem Fahrrad.

Videoclips: Werbung

Und wie immer an dieser Stelle, Werbung aus Deutschland.

Werbung 1
A B C D E F G H I J K L M N O P Q R S T U V **W H K**

Wenn Sie den Kopf voller Ideen haben und immer auf taube Ohren stoßen, der Weg zur WHK ist der beste Schritt zur Selbständigkeit.

Werbung 2
Der echte Scout. Die Nummer 1!

Werbung 3
Es gibt sie also wirklich noch. Die leuchtenden Rapsfelder, die ehrwürdigen alten Alleen, die stillen Wasserlandschaften. Diesen Frieden!

Mecklenburg-Vorpommern. Bilder wie aus einer anderen Zeit. Erleben Sie diese Bilder jetzt im atemberaubend schönen TIME-LIFE-Band *Mecklenburg-Vorpommern*. Rufen Sie gleich an und bestellen Sie diesen Band zehn Tage unverbindlich zur Ansicht. Mecklenburg-Vorpommern ist das Erste von insgesamt 16 Länderporträts aus der neuen großartigen Edition „Die deutschen Länder", mit Reisebeschreibungen bekannter Autoren, mit ausführlichen Berichten über Land und Leute, mit faszinierenden Fotos. Beginnen Sie jetzt diese Edition mit Mecklenburg-Vorpommern, dem Land, das zu den schönsten Deutschlands gehört. Entdecken Sie seine Vielfalt, seinen einzigartigen Reiz, seine packende Faszination, jetzt. Rufen Sie 0130-3232, und sichern Sie sich 150 Seiten schönstes Deutschland im Großformat. Mecklenburg-Vorpommern. Zehn Tage unverbindlich zur Ansicht.

Da bin ich platt!

KAPITEL 2
Spiel und Spaß

Los geht's!

– Hallo, was spielt ihr denn da?
– Was fragst du?
– Ich frage, was ihr da spielt.
– Karten.
– Ja, das sehe ich. Aber was spielt ihr?
– Wir spielen Mau-Mau.
– Wer gewinnt?
– Tara und Ahmet.
– Du gewinnst auch manchmal.
– Aber ihr mogelt oft.
– Was? Wir mogeln nicht!
– Du bist nur sauer, weil du verlierst.
– Spielst du auch Karten, Holger?
– Ja, aber nicht so gern.
– Was machst du denn sonst noch in deiner Freizeit?
– Tja, hm—Fußball, ich geh gern schwimmen, ich ...
– Was noch?
– Im Winter lauf ich Ski.
– Und Hobbys? Hast du andere Interessen?
– Ich sammle Briefmarken, ich höre gern Musik.
– Spielst du ein Instrument?
– Ich spiele Gitarre.
– Prima, und was machst du noch?
– Ja, was noch?
– Spielst du auch Tennis?
– Nein, Tennis spiel ich nicht so gern.
– Ach, das ist schade!
– Warum? Spielst du Tennis?
– Und wie! Mein Lieblingssport!
– Ich ... ich hab ...
– Macht nichts, Holger!
– Ist Holger nett?
– Und wie! Und er läuft Ski, spielt Fußball, aber Tennis spielt er nicht so gern.
– Ach, schade!
– Hallo, Holger!
– Hallo!
– Wir gehen Tennis spielen. Aber schade, du spielst ja Tennis nicht gern! Tschüs!
– He ihr! Wartet doch ... ich ... ich ... So ein Mist!

Fortsetzung

– Hallo!
– Ja?
– Mist!
– Mehr Geduld! Ruhiger musst du spielen!

Kapitel 2 cont.

– Nicht so weit, Mensch!
– Entschuldigung!
– Ja, so ist es besser, Holger!
– Prima!
– Konzentrier dich auf den Ball, Holger!
– Gut, Holger!
– Gut!
– Super, Holger, ganz Klasse! Du spielst schon fast so gut wie Boris Becker!
– Ich?
– Ja, du! Du musst jetzt nur noch ein bisschen aggressiver werden, mutiger spielen, die Bälle höher nehmen.
– Hallo, Holger!
– Hallo!
– Wir gehen Tennis spielen. Aber schade, du magst ja Tennis nicht gern. Tschüs!
– He, ihr, wartet doch! Ich spiele Tennis sehr gerne! Tennis ist prima! Spitze!
– Oh, wirklich? Na, komm! Dann spielen wir heute zusammen.
– Prima, Holger! Ja du lernst wirklich schnell!

Landeskunde (in *Pupil's Edition*)

What kinds of interests do you think German teenagers might enjoy? Here is what some of them told us.

Was machst du gern?

[Michael] Also, ich mach am liebsten in meiner Freizeit Basketballspielen oder ausgehen, so in Diskos oder so was mit Freunden und so und auch Fahrrad fahren.

[Christina] Ich schwimm gern, ich les gern, ich hör gern Musik und ich fahr gern Moped.

[Elke] Ich spiele jetzt gern Volleyball. Im Sommer surf ich, und im Winter geh ich mit meinen Eltern nach Österreich Ski laufen.

[Björn] Tja, ich sitze eigentlich ziemlich oft vor dem Computer. Ich seh auch gern fern oder guck mir ein Video an. Dann fahr ich ganz gerne Rad und schwimme auch manchmal ganz gerne.

[Heide] Ich mach dreimal in der Woche Sport. Da jogg ich vier Kilometer mit Trimm-dich-Pfad, dann fahr ich auch noch Fahrrad danach so eine Stunde mit einem Freund.

Landeskunde (on Video only)

[Johanna] Ich bastle viel und geh zum Jazztanz und spiel Saxophon.

[Melina] Ich, ich spiel gern Tennis, also so halt nur mit Freunden oder so, oder ich geh ins Freibad, jetzt vor allem im Sommer, und Fernsehgucken tu ich auch sehr oft.

[Jasmin] Ich gehe gern schwimmen und dann Eis laufen, und dann fahr ich auch Rollschuh manchmal und noch faulenzen.

[Nicole] Also, ich bin auch Michael Jackson Fan und hör immer seine Musik, und dann spiel ich noch Handball, und Fernsehen schauen halt.

[Jenny] Sport, und ich spiel Keyboard, und ich treff mich gern mit meinen Freunden.

[Tim] Wenn ich relaxen will, leg ich mich aufs Bett und hör Musik, oder ich fahr zu meinem Verein und mach da Fitness-Krafttraining.

[Hermann] Wenn ich Zeit habe, gehe ich segeln, Fahrrad fahren, dann haben wir noch nebenbei einen Garten, da ist ja auch noch viel zu tun, und wir gehen auch spazieren, wir gehen auch ins Kino, ja ...

[Ingo] Ja, meine Hobbys sind eigentlich im weitesten Sinn Computer, also ich bin Computerfan, und ich bin auch in verschiedenen Computerclubs drin, und da programmier ich halt, und im Bereich Datenfernübertragung.

[Anja] Ich geh zu Freunden, ja und geh auch Eis essen, geh ins Kino, quatsch mit denen rum, alber rum.

[Werner] Ja, ich höre Musik, ich lese, ich gehe auf Konzerte, und das war's eigentlich schon.

[Jürgen] Ja, ich geh zum Beispiel Rad fahren, das macht Spaß, gerade die schöne Umgebung kennen lernen, ich organisier Jugendgruppen.

[Dominick] Ich spiel Basketball. Ich lese gerne und spiele Tischtennis.

[Julia] Ja ich mache Sport, ich mach Squash und Fitness, dann lese ich viel, hör Musik.

[Nikki] Ich hör meistens RockSat und ich tanz auch unheimlich gern und tu gern Radfahren.

[Daniela] Ich geh zum Schwimmen und geh immer raus zu meinen Freunden.

Kapitel 2 *cont.*

[Sandra] Also, ich geh gerne ins Kino und in meiner Freizeit spiel ich auch Handball mit der Nicole in einem Verein, und ja sonst also ich sammle auch noch von Macaulay Culkin und sonst eigentlich nichts mehr.

[Thomas] Ich geh auch gern ins Kino, fahr gern Rollschuh und sammle jeden Schnipsel von Jean-Claude van Damme, und das war's dann auch.

Videoclips: Werbung

Und wie immer an dieser Stelle: Werbung aus Deutschland

Werbung 1
Nesfit. Alles ist drin!

Werbung 2
Als wir beschlossen, ein Team zu werden, veränderte sich alles. Das ist mehr, als nur zusammen spielen, das ist, wenn alles verloren scheint, den anderen wieder Mut zu machen, etwas von deiner Stärke zu geben und wieder aufzubauen. Es geht nicht ums Gewinnen. Zusammen für eine Sache ..., darauf kommt es an! Isostar.

Werbung 3
Cebion Plus Magnesium. Es soll dir an nichts fehlen.

Werbung 4
Alpamare.

Werbung 5
Raus ins Freie. Rein in die Natur. Tirol!

KAPITEL 3
Komm mit nach Hause!

Los geht's!

– Du gehst zu Fuß nach Hause? Wo wohnst du denn?
– In der Kopernikusstraße.
– Wo ist die?
– In Babelsberg.
– Ich wohn auch da in der Nähe. Möchtest du mit mir nach Hause kommen?
– Prima!
– Hallo, Mutti! Wo bist du?
– Hier oben! Ich komme gleich runter.
– Das ist Holger, ein Klassenkamerad. Er ist neu.
– Guten Tag, Frau Hartmann!
– Tag, Holger! Möchtet ihr etwas trinken oder was essen?
– Ja, was möchtest du?
– Ach, ich möchte, ich trinke eine Cola.
– Und ich ein Mineralwasser. Haben wir noch Kuchen?
– Ich glaube ja.
– Hier, deine Cola und dein Kuchen.
– Danke!
– Bitte!
– Sag mal, hast du Geschwister?
– Ja, hier, schau! Mein Bruder und meine Schwester.
– Hm, sie sieht nett aus. Wie alt ist sie?
– Bine ist älter. Sie ist neunzehn. Mein Bruder ist zwölf.
– Ach, übrigens, meine Kusine kommt nachher.
– Deine Kusine? Wie alt ist sie?
– So alt wie ich. Auch sechzehn.
– Ja wirklich? Wie sieht sie aus?
– Sie ist sehr hübsch. Sie hat braune Haare, braune Augen. Sie ist einsfünfundsechzig groß und sehr charmant.
– Genau mein Typ.
– Ich weiß! Komm, ich zeig dir jetzt mein Zimmer.
– He! Das Poster! Spitze! Wer ist das?
– Na, rat mal!
– Hm, ich weiß nicht.
– Das ist Patricia Kaas!
– Ach so! Du hast es schön hier. Dein Zimmer ist phantastisch. Die Möbel sind toll! Neu, ja?
– Ja, der Schrank ist neu, das Regal, das Bett und ...
   [*Türklingel*]
– He, das ist bestimmt meine Kusine. Komm mal mit, Holger!

Kapitel 3 *cont.*

- Tag, Jens!
- Tag! Holger, komm mal her!
- Holger: meine Kusine!
- Was? Tara ist deine Kusine? Das glaub ich nicht!
- Ja sicher, ich bin seine Kusine.
- Und ich denke, Tara ist deine Freundin.
- Mensch, Holger! Du denkst zu viel!

Fortsetzung

- Hallo!
- Tag, Tante Monika! Danke für die Zeitschriften. Und die Mutti schickt dir ein paar frische Erdbeeren aus unserem Garten.
- Ja vielen Dank! Ich ruf Mutti dann gleich an.
- Tschüs!
- Prima, also tschüs miteinander.
- Ich glaub, ich gehe auch.
- Wohin gehst du denn?
- Tara, mein lieber Holger, geht jetzt zum Ahmet.
- Zum Ahmet? Wirklich?
- Zu seiner Kusine. Ich helfe ihr mit den Hausaufgaben.
- Was für Fächer?
- Deutsch und Mathe.
- Bist du gut in Mathe?
- Holger, Tara ist ein Genie in Mathe!
- Aber Leute, fahren wir doch alle mal rüber zum Ahmet!
- Prima Idee!
- Ahmets Kusine ist sehr hübsch. Sie hat rot-braune Haare und dunkle Augen.
- Hallo! Hallo! Hallo!
- Die ganze Clique. Hallo!
- Ja, Holger möchte deine Kusine kennen lernen.
- Du spinnst ja, Jens.
- Handan, komm mal her!
- Das ist Holger, er ist neu bei uns.
- Hallo, Holger!
- Hallo, Handan!
- So, genug. Ihr macht jetzt was ihr wollt. Handan und ich, wir lernen jetzt.
- Tschüs!
- Tschüs!
- Und lernt fleißig!

Landeskunde (in *Pupil's Edition*)

We asked several teenagers where they live: **Wo wohnst du?** Here is what they said.

[Dominick] Ich heiß Dominick Klein. Ich bin zwölf Jahre alt und wohn in Hamburg, also Pinneberg, ein Viertel.

[Jasmin] Ich heiße Jasmin und bin fünfzehn. Ich geh in die Reichenau-Schule. Und ich wohne in München, und ich komme aus der Türkei.

[Johanna] Ich heiße Johanna. Ich bin zwölf Jahre alt und ich wohne in Hamburg.

[Thomas] Ich heiße Thomas Schwangart. Ich wohne in München. Ich bin an der Reichenau-Schule und komme aus Italien.

[Ingo] Ja, ich wohn hier in der Nähe, also in der Gustav-Falke-Straße. Das sind zehn Minuten von hier.

Landeskunde (on Video only)

[Jenny] Ich heiße Jenny Steinke. Und ich bin zwölf Jahre alt und wohne in der Hainstraße 3, 2000 Hamburg 20.

[Thorsten] Also, ich heiße Thorsten Weyrauch und bin 14 Jahre alt und ich wohn in Eichwald. Das ist in der Nähe von Esslingen, das ist wieder in der Nähe von Stuttgart.

[Wilhelm] Also, ich heiße Wilhelm Stadler, ich wohn in Eichwald. Das ist in der Nähe von Esslingen und ich bin vierzehn ... fünfzehn Jahre alt.

[Birgit] Ich heiß Birgit, und ich wohn hier in Bietigheim.

[Nikki] Mein Name ist Nikki. Ich bin 13 Jahre alt, und ich gehe in die Reichenau-Schule, und ich komme aus München.

[Gisela] Ich wohne nicht in Hamburg.

Videoclips: Werbung

Und wie immer an dieser Stelle, Werbung aus Deutschland

Werbung 1
Apfel-Botschaft Bodensee.

Werbung 2
- Zur feinen Lebensart gehört es, meine Liebe, immer auf das Original zu achten.

Kapitel 3 *cont.*

– Sehr wohl.

– Auf uns, meine Liebe!

– Ich bewundere deinen Lebensstil, Oliver!

– Trink das Original!

Werbung 3
Apollinaris

Werbung 4
Erleben Sie jetzt den unvergleichlichen Pom-Bär! Pom-Bär, der bärenstarke Kartoffelsnack, ist so kartoffelknusprig verführerisch. Pom-Bär ist immer der beste Knabberfreund. Pom-Bär Original und Pom-Bär Pep. Pom-Bär von Wolf-Bergstraße. Der erste Wolf, der backen kann.

Werbung 5
Wie machst du es denn mit Goldfischli? Mit einer speziellen Knabbertechnik.

Das ist wirklich eine starke Nummer! Wir sind ja auch vom Goldfischli-Fanclub. Knabberdiddu! Wolf-Bergstraße. Der erste Wolf, der backen kann.

Werbung 6
Mit dem BHW kommen Sie früher ins eigene Haus als Sie denken. Finanzieren mit BHW Sofortgeld, Bausparen mit BHW Depot 2000! So packen Sie's! BHW: Ideen für mehr Lebensqualität.

LOCATION OPENER: Schleswig-Holstein

Hallo! Willkommen in Schleswig-Holstein, in der Stadt Wedel. Ich heiße Julia Russek und gehe in die neunte Klasse in das Johann-Rist-Gymnasium. Ich möchte euch jetzt meine Heimat zeigen, die Stadt Wedel und ihre Umgebung. Also, kommt mit!

Wedel liegt an der Elbe. Hier ist das Schulauer Fährhaus mit seiner Schiffsbegrüßungsanlage „Willkomm Höft". Große Schiffe, die hier nach Hamburg vorbeifahren, werden offiziell begrüßt und die Nationalhymne des Heimatlandes wird gespielt. Hier kommt gerade die „Hamburg" vorbei.

Das historische Zentrum Wedels liegt am Marktplatz. Jeden Mittwoch und Freitag findet hier der Wochenmarkt statt.

Das ist das Geburtshaus von Ernst Barlach, dem großen Bildhauer. Das Haus ist heute ein Museum.

Die Wassermühle mit dem Mühlenteich.

Der Roland, der Anker, das Reepschlägerhaus sind die Wahrzeichen Wedels.

So eine Dampferfahrt macht natürlich schon viel Spaß.

Das ist der Hamburger Jachthafen. Hier liegen über 1500 Sportboote.

Ja, Bootfahren auf der Elbe macht schon großen Spaß.

Unser Freibad, das von Mai bis September geöffnet ist.

Ein beliebtes Ausflugsziel ist Fährmanns Sand in der Wedeler Marsch.

In dieser Gegend: Viehzucht und Obstanbau.

Wir können in Wedel auch ins Theater gehen. Die „Batavia" ist ein Theaterschiff.

Hallo! Hier bin ich wieder, und diesmal mit meinen Freunden. Gleich seht und hört ihr mehr über uns. Also, tschüs, bis bald!

KAPITEL 4
Alles für die Schule!

Los geht's!

– Hallo, Leute!
– Hallo, Lars!
– Danke für die Einladung zur Fete!
– Schön, dass du kommst.
– Suchst du was?
– Ja, wo ist der Stundenplan? Sag, wann haben wir Mathe?
– Weiß nicht.
– Ah, Mathe haben wir nach der Pause um 9 Uhr 45.
– Danke, Alex! Und was haben wir heute zuerst?
– Zuerst haben wir Deutsch, dann Bio, danach Mathe, dann English und zuletzt Sport.
– Los, Leute! Der Unterricht fängt an!
– Guten Morgen!
– Morgen!
– Du, heute bekommen wir die Mathearbeit zurück.
– So, hier hab ich eure Arbeiten!
– Ich hab bestimmt wieder eine Vier.
– Meinst du?
– Ja, leider. In Mathe hab ich immer schlechte Noten.

Kapitel 4 *cont.*

– Schade!
– Na ja, du bist gut in Mathe.
– Ja, ich hab Mathe gern. Das ist mein Lieblingsfach.
– Hallo, Lars!
– Hallo, Julia!
– Na, was machst du denn hier? Ach, ich seh's: ein Taschenrechner!
– Schau mal! Der Rechner ist toll, nicht?
– Ja, du hast Recht.
– Und der ist nicht teuer.
– Stimmt! Nur sechzehn Euro! Entschuldigung! Wo sind bitte die Hefte und die Bleistifte?
– Die sind da drüben.
– Und Wörterbücher? Wo sind die?
– Da hinten!
– Danke!
– Der Rechner? Sechzehn Euro, bitte!
– Moment! Ach, wie blöd! Jetzt hab ich nur zehn Euro dabei.
– Macht nichts, Lars! Ich geb dir das Geld.
– Oh, das ist sehr nett, Julia. So, jetzt hab ich zwanzig Euro.
– Danke schön! Und vier Euro zurück.
– Danke!
– Bitte sehr! Auf Wiedersehen!
– Auf Wiedersehen!
– Wiedersehen!
– Ich fahr jetzt nach Hause.
– Ich auch.
– Tschüs!
– Tschüs!
– Warte, Julia!
– Was ist los?
– So ein Mist! Das ganze Zeug auf der Straße!
– Der Taschenrechner, geht er noch?
– Ach wo! Er ist kaputt! So ein Pech!
– So ein Glück! Die Brille ist noch ganz!
– So, was machen wir jetzt?

Fortsetzung

– Tag!
– Tag! Hast du was vergessen?
– Nein. Mein Zeug ist aus der Tasche gefallen, und jetzt ist der Rechner kaputt.
– Zeig mal! Der hat noch keine Batterien!
– Was? Keine Batterien?
– Die muss man immer extra kaufen.
– Ach so! Na prima! Wie viel kosten denn die Batterien?
– Vier Stück, drei Euro sechzig.
– Hast du noch etwas Geld für mich?
– Natürlich, Lars! Hier.

– Danke!
– Drei Euro sechzig und vierzig Cent sind vier Euro und sechs Euro sind zehn. Bitte!
– Danke!
– Bitte! Tschüs!
– Hallo, Sina! Du bist auch da?
– Ja. Und sieh mal, was ich hier habe!
– Das sind drei Hefte zu sechzig Cent, ein Wörterbuch, fünf Euro und vierzig Cent, der Kuli kostet zwei Euro neunzig, zwei Bleistifte zu fünfundvierzig Cent, sechs Farbstifte zu fünfzig Cent, und der Radiergummi kostet siebzig Cent. Macht zusammen vierzehn Euro siebzig.
– Danke! — Vierzehn siebzig und dreißig sind fünfzehn, sechzehn, achtzehn, zwanzig. — Möchtest du eine Tüte?
– Nein, danke. Das geht schon so. — Tschüs!
– Auf Wiedersehen!
– Was macht ihr jetzt?
– Ich fahre nach Hause, Hausaufgaben machen, für Englisch lernen. Morgen haben wir die Englischarbeit.
– Ach ja, das stimmt!
– Ich fahre auch nach Hause.
– Du bekommst noch Geld von mir, vier Euro für den Taschenrechner und drei sechzig für die Batterien — das macht zusammen sieben Euro sechzig.
– Das Geld kannst du mir morgen in der Schule geben. Tschüs!
– Tschüs!
– Tschüs!

Landeskunde (in *Pupil's Edition*)

We asked several teenagers what school subjects they have, and which ones they like and don't like. Here is what some of them said. **Was sind deine Lieblingsfächer?**

[Jasmin] Ich hab Arbeitslehre als Lieblingsfach, und Kunst und Mathe mag ich gar nicht; Physik mag ich auch nicht so gerne. Und sonst, Sport mag ich noch und dann Englisch, das mag ich auch, das ist auch mein Lieblingsfach, weil ich sehr gern Englisch lernen will. Und sonst hab ich keines mehr.

[Michael] Also, ich interessier mich hauptsächlich für Mathe und Physik und Kunst, weil ich also ich Architekt werden will. Und weil die Bereiche sind ... bei Chemie ... ich Chemie überhaupt nicht mag. Ich glaube, es ist auch wichtig. Sonst komm ich mit den meisten Fächern eigentlich zurecht.

Kapitel 4 *cont.*

[Dirk] Also, ich bin eigentlich genau das Gegenteil von ihm, weil ich total auf Sprachen mich basier. Ich hab Englisch-Leistungskurs, Spanisch, Französisch gehabt und so weiter, und will ja auch mit Sprachen später mal was machen, Diplomatie oder so. Mal sehen. Wer weiß?

[Lugana] Okay, ich heiße Lugana, bin Griechin, wurde hier geboren, bin 16 Jahre, gehe aufs Ellental-Gymnasium, und Lieblingsfächer sind Englisch und Deutsch.

[Björn] In der Schule mag ich am liebsten Physik, Mathematik und Informatik, das ist mit Computern. Es kommt, weil ich bin gut in Mathe, ich arbeite gern an Computern, und ich mag Physik ganz gerne, weil mich die Themen einfach interessieren.

[Jenny] Englisch und Sport.

Landeskunde (on Video only)

[Dominick] Sport, Deutsch, Erdkunde.

[Wilhelm] Also, ich geh wie er auf die Realschule Oberesslingen. Also, ich hab auch die Fächer so Deutsch, Geschichte, Gemeinschaftskunde, Sport, Biologie und so weiter, und mein Lieblingsfach ist Geschichte, weil ... da erfährt man mehr über also über unsere Vorfahren und so.

[Nikki] Mein Lieblingsfach ist Geschichte, und Mathe mag ich überhaupt nicht.

[Thomas] Mein Lieblingsfach ist Sport; Mathe mag ich auch nicht.

[Sandra] Mein Lieblingsfach ist auch Sport, und ich mag auch gerne Mathe und die anderen, also, Geschichte und Biologie und so die Fächer mag ich auch noch gerne.

[Maren] Also, ich gehe aufs Gymnasium im Ellental und meine Lieblingsfächer sind Sport, Bio und BK.

[Bianca] Also, Erdkunde, Biologie, Sport, BK halt, Deutsch, Mathe, Englisch. Meine Lieblingsfächer: Mathe und Sport.

[Thomas] Meine Lieblingsfächer: Biologie und Englisch und Sport.

[Johannes] Also, welche Fächer ich nicht gern hab, sind Mathematik und Deutsch, und am liebsten habe ich eigentlich Biologie und Sport, ja.

[Marco] Also, meine Lieblingsfächer sind Deutsch und Biologie, und Mathe mag ich überhaupt nicht.

[Iwan] Also, ich bin Iwan Dudic, bin 16 Jahre alt und gehe hier aufs Ellental-Gymnasium in Bietigheim, und meine Lieblingsfächer sind Mathematik und Physik und Biologie. Und ein Fach, das ich nicht so gern mag, wär' Chemie.

[Elke] Mein Lieblingsfach ist Biologie und Sport, und jetzt mach ich ganz neu Darstellendes Spielen.

[Ria] Meins ist Darstellendes Spielen, Biologie und Sport.

[Jens] Meine Lieblingsfächer sind Physik, Sport und Darstellendes Spielen. Was ich überhaupt nicht mag ist Deutsch. Weil ... die Grammatik ist schwer, und die Arbeiten sind auch ziemlich hart.

[Jasmin] Äh, Kunst, Kunst und Kunst und Erdkunde.

[Roland] Sport und Mathe hab ich sehr gerne, hab ich auch als Leistungskurse gewählt. Und Englisch und Deutsch mag ich nicht sehr gerne. Warum nicht? Liegt mir nicht so gut, das kann ich auch nicht so gut.

[Jochen] Ja, bei mir ist das Mathe und Deutsch, mochte ich immer gern, schon als kleines Kind, rechnen und auch in Deutsch ... wir diskutieren über Texte und analysieren und das gefällt mir ganz gut, und was mir nicht so gut gefällt ist Englisch und Geschichte eigentlich, aber das liegt auch an den Lehrern.

[Annike] Ich bin Annike Heizig, ich bin 16 und ich gehe auf das Helene-Lange-Gymnasium, das ist ein zweisprachiges Gymnasium Englisch/Deutsch, und ja meine Lieblingsfächer sind so Sprachen halt, Englisch, Französisch und Musik und Kunst.

[Fabian] Ja, also ich bin Fabian Schacht, 16, gehe aufs Bismarck-Gymnasium, habe als erste Fremdsprache Englisch gekriegt, und mein Lieblingsfach ist auch Englisch, sonst mag ich noch Bio und Chemie. Und was ich eigentlich absolut hasse ist Physik.

[Melanie] Lieblingsfächer habe ich an sich keine weiter. Naturwissenschaften mag ich nicht so gerne. So Mathe, Physik und Chemie, mag ich nicht so gern, aber mehr so Fächer wie Deutsch zum Beispiel. Wenn man da Bücher liest und dann über diese Bücher spricht, das ist dann schon ganz gut.

Kapitel 4 cont.

[Katja] Na ja, ich mag eigentlich lieber die Naturwissenschaften, Mathematik oder Physik und Chemie, weil ich das besser verstehe als jetzt Sprachen; da bin ich auch nicht so gut drin. Und deshalb mach ich jetzt lieber so was wie Rechnen.

Videoclips: Werbung

Und wie immer an dieser Stelle, Werbung aus Deutschland!

Werbung 1
Haben Sie schon mal einen fröhlicheren Schulranzen gesehen als den Micky-Maus-Schulranzen von Herlitz?

Herlitz: eine Idee voraus!

Werbung 2
Ollie braucht sie eigentlich nicht, die Rückenpolsterung vom neuen Joker-System. Das Schloss, das ihr mit einer Hand aufmachen könnt. Reflektoren hat er natürlich auch, damit ihr sicher unterwegs seid. Vor allem kann man ihn auseinander bauen, das ist echt gut, denn deshalb kann man ihn später recyceln. Ihr könnt ihn waschen, und was noch besser ist, es gibt die absolut überstarken Motive zum Wechseln, mit denen euch die tollsten Sachen passieren können. Joker System solltet ihr euch echt merken!

Werbung 3
Schreibunterlagen mit Pfiff.

Werbung 4
Papierkörbe für alle Fälle.

Holen Sie sich einen Korb.

KAPITEL 5
Klamotten kaufen

Los geht's!

– Ach ja! Die Fete morgen!
– Was ziehst du denn zu Sonjas Fete an? Rock? Pulli?
– Ach was! Ich zieh meinen Jogging-Anzug an.
– Und ich meine Shorts. Ich brauche aber etwas, 'ne Bluse oder ein T-Shirt. Das ist zu alt und gefällt mir nicht.
– Und ich brauche ein Stirnband für meine Haare. Komm, gehen wir zum Sport-Kerner!
– Prima Idee!
– Schau, der Michael!
– Hallo, ihr beiden!
– Was hast du denn da in der Tüte?
– Na, wie gefällt euch mein T-Shirt?
– Mensch, scheußlich!
– Wirklich? Also, ich finde es stark!
– Na, wie du meinst. Tschüs!
– Guten Tag!
– Guten Tag!
– Haben Sie einen Wunsch?
– Ich suche eine Bluse.
– Blusen haben wir in allen Größen und allen Farben. Hier haben wir etwas für Sie: Toll, nicht?
– Haben Sie auch Blusen in Blau?
– Natürlich! Hier, in Blau, Größe 40. Passt bestimmt.
– Probier doch mal an!
– Sehr sportlich. Und sie passt dir gut.
– Meinst du? Ach, weißt du, nein. Die Bluse gefällt mir nicht!
– Haben Sie T-Shirts? In Blau oder lieber in Weiß?
– Hier habe ich T-Shirts. Sehr sportlich, sehr schick.
– Schau mal, Katja! Ein T-Shirt mit Aufdruck!
– Ein Texas-Motiv. Das ist toll!
– Das ist aber zu groß für Sie. Sie brauchen M, medium.
– Ist das aus Baumwolle?
– Hundert Prozent Baumwolle.
– Prima! Das probier ich mal an.
– Phantastisch, Katja. Das finde ich echt toll! Lässig. Weiß ist eine gute Farbe für dich.
– Tja, du weißt, Weiß ist meine Lieblingsfarbe. Was kostet das T-Shirt?
– Einundzwanzig Euro fünfzig.
– Was, so viel? Das ist teuer.
– Das hat halt nicht jeder. Ein spitze T-Shirt!

Kapitel 5 *cont.*

– Na ja, wer schön sein will, muss zahlen, nicht?
– Das ist toll für die Fete. Gut, ich nehme es.

Fortsetzung

– Ja, dieses T-Shirt in Weiß mit diesem Motiv.
– Na prima! Ich möchte ... wir möchten auch dieses T-Shirt kaufen.
– Äh, auch in Weiß.
– Bitte.
– Danke!
– Wiedersehen!
– Wiedersehen!
– Wiedersehen! Vielen Dank!
– Ah, schön, dass ihr da seid!
– Wie findest du Katjas T-Shirt? Fesch, nicht?
– Du, es ist nicht das erste Mal, dass ich heute das T-Shirt sehe.
– So? Na, nein das ist schick, einzigartig.
– Hallo Katja!
– Das darf doch nicht wahr sein!
– Komm her zu uns! Gleich zu Gleich gesellt sich gern!
– Mensch, Michael, das finde ich echt gemein!
– Was heißt gemein? Komm her, shake hands!
– Cheese!
– Hallo!

Landeskunde (in *Pupil's Edition*)

What do you think German students usually like to wear when they go to a party? We asked them: **Welche Klamotten sind „in"?**

[Sandra] Also, wenn ich zu einer Party gehe, dann ziehe ich am liebsten Jeans an und vielleicht einen Body und einen weiten Pulli da drüber, meistens dann etwas in Blau oder 'nen weißen Pulli, jetzt wie grad eben, aber Lieblingsfarbe ist doch Blau, und Weiß.

[Alexandra] Ja, ich ziehe am liebsten Jeans an, und Lieblingsfarben sind dann so Blau oder Pastellfarben, und auf Partys oder so eigentlich immer in Jeans und mal was Schöneres oben. Disko ist dann auch, na, ab und zu hab ich mal gern einen Rock.

[Melina] Am liebsten mag ich Jeans, vor allem helle, oder ja so lockere Blusen, kurze halt, und jetzt vor allem T-Shirts, einfarbige. Und sie sollen halt schön lang sein und ein bisschen locker. Und ja, meine Lieblingsfarben sind Blau, Apricot, oder Rot, Lila auch noch. Ja, das wär's.

[Iwan] Also, wenn ich auf eine Party gehe, ziehe ich am liebsten ein T-Shirt an und eine kurze Hose. Am liebsten trage ich Schwarz, so einfach, weil es halt schön aussieht und weil es bequem ist.

Landeskunde (on Video only)

[Gabi] Ja, normalerweise doch Jeans, aber vielleicht ein bisschen was Ausgefalleneres dazu, schöne Schuhe, andere Frisur, es kommt darauf an.

[Anja] Also, nicht so superschick, nicht so wie in die Oper, aber schon nicht so wie in die Schule. Also, schon Jeans, aber ein bisschen feiner auch, bisschen besser als der normale Alltag.

[Jürgen] Also, wenn ich zu einer Fete gehe, dann ziehe ich normalerweise Jeans in allen Farben an, dazu T-Shirts, die farblich passen, und, na ja, versuche eher locker, lässig mich zu kleiden.

[Susanne] Ich trage am liebsten Freizeitmode, weil es am bequemsten ist.

[Frau Troger] Für die Arbeit, Dirndlkleider, für Sport und Freizeit sportliche, ein bissel locker.

[Gerhard] In meiner Freizeit ziehe ich am liebsten Jeans, T-Shirt, zum Arbeiten habe ich immer schwarzweiß, da trägt man da in der Freizeit lieber was Bequemes.

[Markus] Am liebsten in der Freizeit Jeans, leichte Kleidung, und 'ne leichte Lederjacke, nicht so gezwungen, keinen Schlips, keine Krawatte. Locker, fröhlich.

[Lore] Ich trage am liebsten sportliche Kleidung: Jeanshosen und T-Shirts, und auch aber schon mal gerne Kleider, so jetzt im Sommer leichte Blusen und Röcke und Sandalen.

[Lugana] Wenn ich auf eine Fete gehe, dann kommt es darauf an. Wenn die Leute sehr edel angezogen sind, dann ziehe ich mich auch so an, und wenn sie nicht so wenn sie normal angezogen sind, dann ziehe ich mich auch so an. Und Lieblingsfarben sind Schwarz, Rot und Weiß.

[Birgit] Ja, also ich ziehe meistens 'ne Jeans an und dann noch ein Oberteil, ein T-Shirt oder so, und meine Lieblingfarbe ist Dunkelgrün.

[Johannes] Eigentlich das, was ich gerade anhab, kurze Hose, T-Shirt, eigentlich ganz locker, Turnschuhe oder Docks.

German 1 Komm mit! — Video Guide

Kapitel 5 *cont.*

[Gerd] Am liebsten halt ein schwarzes T-Shirt und 'ne halblange Hose oder 'ne dreiviertelslange Hose, das ist einfach am bequemsten und sieht am besten aus.

[Eva] Also ich mag, bei Kleidung mag ich am liebsten so Cordhosen, weil die schön billig sind, und da ich nicht so viel Geld habe, kaufe ich mir auch mehr billige Sachen. Und Lieblingsfarbe ist Schwarz.

[Monika] Also, ich zieh gerne Jeans an und bequeme T-Shirts, also eigentlich alles Mögliche, was bequem ist, wo man sich drin wohl fühlt. Meine Lieblingsfarbe ist Lila und Schwarz.

[Werner] Ja, ich trage am liebsten Jeans und T-Shirts, würde ich sagen. Also, so wie jetzt zum Beispiel.

[Michael] Also bei mir bei Jeans mag ich nur Schwarz oder Blau; ich mag nicht so knallige Farben. Und sonst, ja was gerade da ist, okay. Ich kauf so Sachen, die ich mag, oder ich geb lieber ein bisschen mehr Geld dafür aus, und trag es öfter, anstatt viel zu haben, und es nicht so oft zu tragen. Also, mir ist es eigentlich egal.

[Dirk] Ja, ich bin auch total konservativ in den Farben. Ich bin nicht so für Hellblau, Giftgrün, oder so 'ne Sache sondern normal; einfach Pulli, Jeans, und dann hat's sich. Einfach irgendwas, wo man aufsteht, und dann packt's rauf und dann geht man zur Schule. Ist ja nur zur Schule. Wochenende ist es anders.

Videoclips: Werbung

Und wie immmer an dieser Stelle, Werbung aus Deutschland.

Werbung 1
He, wer ist denn die mit dem Kleid? Die sieht ja wahnsinnig aus. He, kommt die hierher? Ich glaub, die kommt wirklich hierher ... das darf doch nicht ... ich werd verrückt!
– Du sag mal, bist du nicht Richard?
– Wer ist Richard? Egal! Ja!
– Die Damenmode. Im neuen Quelle Katalog.

Werbung 2
Genau, das grüne Kleid, geht das auch bis morgen? Mode im 24-Stunden-Takt. Jetzt bei OTTO.

Werbung 3
Persil Color—Reinheit mit Colorschutz.

Erst habe ich das im Fernsehen gesehen, da dachte ich, na ja, Reinheit und Farbschönung! Erzählen können die ja viel. Aber als dann Chris wieder mal, wie jetzt, völlig verdreckt nach Hause kam, hab ich mir gedacht, Versuchst du es mal—holst du dir Persil Color!

Ja, das Color von Persil. Dem traute ich es am ehesten zu, dass es wirklich die Farben schützt und gleichzeitig den Schmutz rauswäscht. Ich war total gespannt.

Normale Vollwaschmittel sind farbenblind. Persil Color mit Colorschutz erkennt die Farben und wäscht farbrein sauber, fast wie sortiert. Die Hose—wieder richtig sauber und die Farben absolut frisch—und beides zugleich: toll!

Persil Color wäscht farbrein sauber!

Werbung 4
Servus, Ottie, pack 'mer's wieder! Neu in dieser Saison: Hypercolor. Wie unser bezauberndes Model zeigt, wechselt Hypercolor bei Wärme die Farbe. In allen Größen. So ein Schmarr'n! Die verrücktesten Klamotten, seit es Chamäleons gibt. Hypercolor!

Werbung 5
Phantastisch deine Bluse. Ist die neu?

Nein, mit Perwoll gewaschen. Das ist die Idee!

So viel Schönheit. Die muss neu sein.

Nein, mit Perwoll gewaschen mit Weichpfleger.

Man lernt nie aus!

Du hast einen Sinn fürs Schöne. Ist sie neu?

Nein, mit Perwoll gewaschen.

Das ist wahre Kunst!

Perwoll und Perwoll flüssig, damit es Schmusewolle bleibt.

KAPITEL 6
Pläne machen

Los geht's!

- Hallo Heiko! Wie geht's denn so?
- Hm ... So lala. Was machst du jetzt so hier? Wohin gehst du?
- Zu Katja. Wir machen zuerst Hausaufgaben, und dann wollen wir ins Café Freizeit gehen, ein Eis essen. Willst du mitkommen?
- Gern! Wann wollt ihr gehen?
- Wie spät ist es jetzt?
- Viertel nach drei.
- Ja, so um halb fünf?
- Ok.
- Bis dann, tschüs!
- Tschüs!
- Hallo! Hierher!
- Du Michael, dein neuer Haarschnitt ist super!
- Nicht zu kurz?
- Nein, überhaupt nicht.
- Ehrlich?
- Ehrlich!
- Guten Tag! Was bekommt ihr?
- Ich bekomme einen Eisbecher. Fruchteis.
- Ich möchte einen Cappuccino, bitte.
- Hm ... ich will im Moment gar nichts. Ich esse später etwas.
- Und ich esse jetzt eine Pizza. Nummer eins, bitte.
- Cappuccino?
- Ich bekomme den. Er ist für mich! Danke!
- Eisbecher?
- Den Eisbecher bekomme ich.
- Bitte sehr!
- Danke!
- Die Pizza kommt gleich.
- Schon gut!
- Milch, Katja?
- Da ist schon Milch drin, danke. Aber Zucker bitte!
- Gern.
- Danke!
- Bitte!
- Eine Pizza, bitte. Guten Appetit!
- Danke!
- Noch einen Wunsch?
- Nein, danke!
- Schmeckt's, Michael?
- Und wie, sagenhaft! Willst du mal probieren?
- Ja gern! Hm, sie ist wirklich gut.
- Was du so alles essen kannst!
- Der Appetit kommt beim Essen!
- Man ist, was man isst, mein lieber Michael!
- Bitte?
- Ich möchte zahlen, bitte!
- Eine Pizza, drei Euro. Ein Wurstbrot, zwei Euro 60. Eine Cola, ein Euro 50. Macht zusammen sieben Euro zehn, bitte.
- Danke! Auf Wiedersehen!
- Wiedersehen! Und nun trinke ich meine Cola aus und gehe.
- Du! Pass doch auf!
- Oje! Katja, es tut mir Leid.
- Macht ja nichts! Es ist ja nur mein T-Shirt!

Fortsetzung

- Schade, das schöne T-Shirt.
- Das kann man waschen. Der Fleck geht bestimmt wieder raus!
- Na klar!
- Hallo!
- Ich komme sofort. Bitte?
- Ich möchte jetzt etwas essen. Die Nudelsuppe bitte.
- Und für mich ein Wasser.
- Ja, und für mich auch eins.
- Alles?
- Ja.
- Der Kellner ist immer sehr nett.
- Stimmt. Der kennt uns schon.
- Er sieht gut aus.
- Mir gefallen seine Augen und ...
- Eine Suppe!
- Danke!
- Und zwei Wasser.
- Danke!
- Danke!
- Bitte sehr.
- Schau mal Katja, wer da kommt!
- Das ist doch—das kann doch nicht wahr sein!
- Meine liebe Katja, es tut mir wirklich Leid. Hier, ein paar Blumen für dich!
- Das ist sehr lieb, Michael. Danke. Jetzt bin ich wirklich nicht mehr sauer.
- Ehrlich?
- Ehrlich!

Landeskunde (in *Pupil's Edition*)

What do you think students in Germany like to do when they have time to spend with their friends? Here is what some of them told us.

Was machst du in deiner Freizeit?

[Sandra] Also, meine Freizeit verbringe ich am

Kapitel 6 cont.

liebsten mit ein paar Freundinnen oder Freunden. Dann gehen wir abends in die Stadt, essen Eis, oder wir gehen tanzen, oder wir setzen uns einfach in ein Café rein und reden. Aber am liebsten gehen wir halt tanzen.

[Annika] Also, ich mach auch nicht so viel mit meinen Eltern. Ich bin bei den Pfadfindern; da fährt man halt am Wochenende auf Fahrt, und ja, mit denen mach ich auch hauptsächlich ziemlich viel, auch mal außerhalb, also abends weggehen, ins Kino gehen und so, mach ich dann auch mit den Pfadfindern, und dann spiel ich noch Klavier.

[Marga] Ja, das ist sehr unterschiedlich. Wenn ich heimkomme, mach ich eigentlich erst einmal meine Hausaufgaben, dann gehe ich noch mit Freunden weg, oder spiel Tennis und Gitarre, ja und ich mach auch Ballet und tänzerisch sehr viel. Ja, da ist meine Freizeit schon ausgebucht.

[Karsten] Also, ich mach als Erstes natürlich Hausaufgaben, notgedrungen, und dann ja entweder irgendwas mit Sport, oder geh in die Stadt einkaufen, oder meistens treff ich mich mit meiner Freundin.

Landeskunde (on Video only)

[Paolo] Also, in meiner Freizeit probe ich für das Modetheater Überlingen, Laufmode, und ansonsten mache ich ein bisschen Bodybuilding und Kickboxen, als Kampfsportart.

[Jasmin] In meiner Freizeit tanze ich gern mit Freunden, da versammeln wir uns immer und wir hören gern Musik, also Michael Jackson, der ist mein Lieblingsstar, den höre ich schon seit acht Jahren, und gehen auch schwimmen; und Eislaufen mag ich gerne; und dann noch Rollschuhfahren und immer ausgehen.

[Lore] Ich bin gerne mit Freunden unterwegs, und wir fahren dann Fahrrad, oder ich gehe viel spazieren und wandern, fahre gern in Urlaub, solche Sachen.

[Ute] Ich gehe schwimmen, spiele Akkordeon, fahre meine Freunde am Moped, oder andere Dinge.

[Lugana] In meiner Freizeit spiele ich gerne Basketball, fahre gerne Fahrrad, Volleyball und Federball.

[Bianca] Ich reite und ich schwimme.

[Johannes] Oh, am liebsten Tennis, Judo, mit Freunden wohin gehen, Freibad, lesen, und ja Fahrrad fahren, Schlittschuh fahren, alles Mögliche, Ski fahren, eigentlich alles.

[Gerd] Ich fahre Skateboard, das macht mir halt Spaß, ist ein netter Zeitvertreib.

[Alexandra] Ja, bei mir läuft's eigentlich fast gleich ab. Ich spiel auch Tennis und auch Gitarre, ich mach dann noch Jazz und sonst so nach der Schule, mache ich vielleicht 'ne Stunde überhaupt nichts, und dann mache ich Hausaufgaben. Na, und sonst verbleibt eigentlich nicht mehr viel.

[Stefan] Ja, ich treibe ein wenig Sport und geh ab und zu ins Kino, ins Museum, oder mit meiner Freundin ja, Theater.

[Werner] Ja, ich höre Musik. Ich lese. Ich gehe auf Konzerte. Und das wär's eigentlich schon.

[Jochen] Ich spiele gerne Basketball im Verein, in einer Mannschaft, bin Schiedsrichter, trainiere eine kleine Jungen-Mannschaft, weil es sehr viel Spaß macht, kleinen Kindern was beizubringen, vor allem in einem Sport, der mir selber auch sehr gut gefällt, weil er abwechslungsreich ist und immer was los ist dabei.

[Dirk] Ich? Normalerweise snowboarde ich. In Hamburg gibt es keine Snowboard-Möglichkeiten, leider. Ansonsten auch nur so Squash und solche Sachen. Sonst würde ich auf die Piste gehen am Wochenende.

[Monika] Ich gehe auf Konzerte, treffe mich mit Freunden, gehe Billiard spielen und, na, ich hab auch ein Pferd, und das beansprucht natürlich auch viel Zeit. Insofern muss man da schon sehen, wie man damit zurechtkommt.

[Herta] Ich hab eigentlich kaum Zeit. Ich hab bis vier Schule und wenn ich dann fertig bin, muss ich noch Hausaufgaben machen. Wenn ich damit fertig bin, geh ich arbeiten. Das dauert bis halb elf, und wenn ich dann nach Hause komme, weil es ist so lange von der Arbeit bis nach Hause, muss ich dann gleich schlafen. Also, es lohnt sich nicht, irgendetwas zu machen. Am Wochenende treff ich mich mit meinen Freunden oder geh irgendwohin weg oder so, viel Zeit hab ich gar nicht.

[Melanie] Während der Woche verabrede ich mich an sich nicht so oft, weil ich da ziemlich viel mit der Schule zu tun hab, Hausaufgaben und so. Aber sonst am Wochenende gehe ich eben abends weg, ins Kino oder in die Disko, oder wenn Vereinsveranstaltungen sind, geht man dahin. Und sonst tanze ich, und einmal in der Woche hab ich auch Flöte, also Musik mach ich da noch ein bisschen.

Kapitel 6 cont.

[Katja] Ja, bei mir ist es eigentlich genauso. Während der Woche habe ich fast nie Zeit, irgendwas zu unternehmen, mit Freunden oder so, weil man so viel mit der Schule zu tun hat, Hausaufgaben, und ansonsten eben auch tanzen und am Wochenende eben mit Freunden verabreden oder in die Disko gehen, oder eben auch tanzen.

Videoclips: Werbung

Und wie immer an dieser Stelle: Werbung aus Deutschland

Werbung 1
Ich hab die absolut genaue Zeit. Das ist eine Funkuhr von Junghans. Die geht immer auf die Sekunde genau. Funkgesteuert. Sie stellt sich sogar automatisch von Sommerzeit auf Winterzeit um. Das ist das Neueste, was es gibt. Richtig, denn das Allerneueste sind die Junghans-Mega-Funkuhren für Damen.

Junghans: Uhren mit Ideen

Werbung 2
Ja, det isse Original Wagner-Pizza aus dem modernen Steinbackofen. Knusperdünner Boden und oben ja, mächtig watt druff! Und jetzt bist dran!

Original Wagner-Pizza. Einmal Wagner, immer Wagner.

Werbung 3
Sacher — der Anfang einer großen Leidenschaft. Sacher-Eiskrem. Viel frische Sahne macht es so traumhaft sahnig.

Traumhaft sahnig. Sacher—der Anfang einer großen Leidenschaft.

Werbung 4
Bleib fit, rein ins volle Leben, los geht's! Lass die anderen stehen. Und wenn dann der große Durst kommt, trink doch einfach Überkinger. Spür die Kraft der Mineralien. Fühl dich einfach Überkinger!

LOCATION OPENER: München

Grüß Gott! Willkommen in München, in der Hauptstadt Bayerns. Ich heiße Mara Zlinac, bin 15, und besuche hier in München die neunte Klasse der Rudolf-Diesel-Realschule. Nun, ich möchte jetzt nicht über meine Schule reden: nein, etwas ganz anderes. Ich möchte euch München zeigen. Also, auf geht's!

München ist die Hauptstadt Bayerns. In diesem Gebäude dort tagt der Bayerische Landtag.

Dieses Gebäude hier ist ganz neu. Es ist die neue Staatskanzlei der Landesregierung. Von hier aus hat man einen schönen Blick auf den Hofgarten mit der Theatinerkirche.

München hat zwei Wahrzeichen: da ist der Dom mit seinen zwei Türmen, und hier ist das Münchner Kindl, hier am Tor zum Rathaus abgebildet.

Münchens Herz ist der Marienplatz, die gute Stube der Münchner. Hier kann man auf Freunde warten, lesen, essen und auf das Glockenspiel warten. Zweimal am Tag drehen sich die bunten Figuren, die Szenen aus der bayerischen Geschichte zeigen.

Ja, in München ist viel los. Für die Techniker unter euch gibt es das Deutsche Museum. Es ist so groß, dass ihr viele Tage braucht und noch nicht alles seht.

Und für die Künstler unter euch, ja, da gibt es so viele Kunstmuseen. Hier in der Alten Pinakothek hängen europäische Meister aus dem 14. bis 18. Jahrhundert.

Die Meister des 19. Jahrhunderts hängen in der Neuen Pinakothek.

Und Autofreaks gehen natürlich ins BMW-Museum. Und hier gegenüber ist das Olympiagelände; 1972 haben hier die olympischen Sommerspiele stattgefunden.

Ein beliebtes Ausflugsziel der Münchner ist Schloss Nymphenburg, die ehemalige Sommerresidenz der bayerischen Kurfürsten und Könige.

Für Musikliebhaber, und ganz besonders für Fans der Oper, haben wir das Nationaltheater und gleich daneben das Cuvilliéstheater.

Ja, und noch was, unser Englischer Garten, ein beliebtes Ziel für die Fußgänger und Radler.

Hier bin ich auf dem Viktualienmarkt, das ist der älteste und größte Lebensmittelmarkt in München. Hier kann man alles kaufen, aber das will ich ja nicht. Ich suche nämlich meine Freunde.

Hallo, da seid ihr ja!

Hallo!

Das sind meine Schulfreunde. Und bald werdet ihr mehr von uns hören und sehen.

Also, bis dann! Pfüat euch! Servus! Servus!

KAPITEL 7
Zu Hause helfen

Los geht's!

– Claudia, hallo!
– Hallo!
– Servus, Claudia!
– Hallo, Claudia!
– Wohin geht's?
– In den Englischen Garten. Komm doch mit!
– Das geht heute nicht. Ich muss zu Hause helfen.
– Schade, dass du nicht mitkommen kannst! Es ist heute so schönes Wetter zum Radeln.
– Was musst du denn tun, Claudia?
– Ich muss mein Zimmer aufräumen, Müll sortieren, das …
– Einen Moment! Ich hab 'ne Idee. Fahren wir alle zur Claudia und helfen ihr!
– Prima Idee! Ja, dann ist sie schnell fertig und kann mitkommen.
– Das ist lieb von euch!
– Du, was müssen wir jetzt tun?
– Markus, du und der Flori, ihr könnt den Müll sortieren.
– Gern, machen wir!
– Die Flaschen kommen hier rein, die Dosen kommen da rein.
– Die Zeitungen?
– Die Zeitungen kommen in den Korb da.
– Und du, Mara, willst du mir helfen?
– Klar, also los!
– Deine Klamotten musst du selber aufräumen.
– Mach ich schon! Willst du für mich Staub saugen?
– Das muss ich auch immer zu Hause machen.
– So, wir sind fertig.
– Wir auch.
– Also, gehen wir. Die Sonne scheint noch immer.
– Ich muss nur noch die Katze füttern.
– Wer weiß denn, wie morgen das Wetter wird?
– Morgen regnet es.
– Ach Quatsch! Es bleibt schön!
– Was sagt denn der Wetterbericht?
– Weiß nicht. Der stimmt aber sowieso nie!
– Micki! Micki! Wo bist du?
– Ist die Katze schon wieder weg?
– Ja. Sie muss ins Haus.
– Also los, Kinder! Wir müssen die Katze suchen.
– Micki! Micki!

Fortsetzung

– Micki! Micki!
– Miau!
– Hast du die Katze gehört?
– Du warst das. Du hast Miau gemacht!
– Ich?
– Wo ist denn der Flori?
– Miau.
– So, Micki, hier ist dein Futter. Hm, und hier ist was für mich!
– Mensch, da ist ja die Micki. Und du frisst auch Katzenfutter, du Naschkatze!
– Hm, lecker.
 (Telefon)
– Bei Müller! Danke, gut! Ja, er ist da. Mach ich! Tschüs! Deine Mutter.
– Servus, Mami. Was? Das kann nicht sein! Heute ist erst Mittwoch. Ja, dann komm ich gleich vorbei. Tschau! — Jetzt muss ich arbeiten.
– Nicht so schlimm; jetzt helfen wir dir.

(Alle beim Helfen.)
– Mami, wir sind fertig!
– Ja, vielen Dank! Und da ist etwas Gutes für euch.
– Hm, danke!
– Hm, danke! Auf Wiederschau'n!
– Tschau!
– Tschüs, viel Spaß!
– Deine Mutti ist sehr lieb.
– Ist sie auch.
– Mm, riecht gut!
– Das haben wir uns auch verdient.

Landeskunde (in *Pupil's Edition*)

In both the old and new states, Germans today are very aware of the need to protect the environment. Young people all over Germany are involved in projects that range from recycling to cleaning up rivers and forests. Here is what some of them said they do for the environment.

Was tust du für die Umwelt?

[Marga] Also, bei uns zu Hause wird jeder Müll sortiert, eben in Plastik und Aluminium und Papier, und so weiter. Das halten wir eigentlich ziemlich streng ein und ja, wenn es schönes Wetter ist und es sich vermeiden lässt, mit dem Auto zu fahren, nehm ich lieber das Fahrrad und, ja, so denken wir eigentlich schon fortschrittlich und umweltbewusst.

Kapitel 7 *cont.*

[**Fabian**] Also, wir tun für die Umwelt, dass wir einmal also, Müll vermeiden, dass wir unser Altpapier wegbringen, Glas sammeln, und möglichst auch Glas, das wieder verwertet werden kann, kaufen, also, sprich, Mehrwegflaschen und, ja, dass wir halt möglichst wenig Putzmittel oder so, wenn's denn nötig ist, nur im Abguss und im Sparsamen gebrauchen.

[**Elke**] Ja, ich habe mit meinen Eltern angefangen, Flaschen zu sortieren und regelmäßig zum Container zu bringen. Der Müll wird meistens auch separat sortiert und dann, ja, einstweilen weggebracht und sonst, ja, Umwelt, zähl ich dazu, dass man mit dem Bus zur Schule fährt und nicht mit dem Auto und, ja, das wär's.

Landeskunde (on Video only)

[**Margit**] Ich denke, ich bin relativ durchschnittlich umweltbewusst. Ich guck schon darauf, ich versuche möglichst wenig mit dem Auto zu fahren, also Benzin zu sparen, Müll zu trennen, und ein bisschen auf den Wasserverbrauch und Energieverbrauch zu achten.

[**Susanne**] Ich trenne meinen Abfall, so weit möglich. Also hier in München gibt's noch nicht so viele Möglichkeiten, aber Papier, Alu, das mach ich schon, und fahr, wenn möglich, auch mit dem Fahrrad.

[**Herr Troger**] Ja, für die Umwelt, was wir für die Umwelt tun, da kann ich mal sagen, dass wir eine äußerst genaue Mülltrennung, das ist bei uns jetzt sehr gefragt, nicht wahr, eine äußerst genaue Mülltrennung also in die Tonnen, also in die eine Tonne kommt der Hausmüll, der also weggeführt wird, in die andere Tonne kommen die Dosen und dann in die nächste Tonne das Papier und so weiter. Dann wird getrennt noch die Kartons, die geben wir, da haben wir eine eigene Stelle dafür am Gemeindeplatz, da wird das getrennt. Das machen wir also für die Umwelt. Wir haben auch in St. Ulrich eine ganz prima Kanalisierung gemacht, hat uns sehr viel Geld gekostet, aber da haben wir alle einheitlich angeschlossen, nicht wahr? Und somit kann man schon sagen, dass man für die Umwelt einiges tut.

[**Ute**] Ja, also, zum Beispiel Zeitungspapier, also nicht in den normalen Müll sondern, also zur Wiederverwertung in den Spezialmüll, zum Recycling, ja oder halt nicht irgendwas achtlos wegwerfen, sondern zum Müll tragen.

[**Rolf**] Meine Mutter, die sortiert schon so Altpapier und so ... so Zeitungen. Aber ich mach nichts, eigentlich.

[**Johannes**] Ja, hauptsächlich Wasser sparen und Strom sparen eben. Nicht so viel verbrauchen.

[**Marco**] Also, wir tun so Müll sammeln und sortieren und dann recyceln lassen.

[**Sandra**] Also, wir trennen bei uns zu Hause Müll, wir sortieren zum Beispiel Altpapier, da gibt's die extra Container dafür, oder Flaschen, und dann Kompost, also gerade so Grünzeug, Gemüse und so, was Abfall ist, das wird bei uns alles im Garten kompostiert. Und ansonsten versuchen wir, so wenig Müll wie möglich aufkommen zu lassen.

[**Alexandra**] Bei uns wird der Müll auch sortiert—Dosen, Alu, Folie, Papier, Glas. Normalerweise fahren wir auch lieber mit dem Fahrrad. Auto hat halt Katalysator, und, ja, wir bemühen uns halt, wo es geht, Müll zu vermeiden. Wir kompostieren auch Müll.

[**Eva**] Ja, im Haushalt, eben sortieren Flaschen, Plastik, Papier.

[**Ria**] Ja, bei uns fängt es auch schon bei den ganzen Putzmitteln halt an, und zu Hause, dass wir halt umweltfreundliche Sachen benutzen. Und die Zeitungen werden dann halt auch gesammelt, und Flaschen und so werden halt auch weggebracht in den Container.

[**Jens**] Also, ich achte beim Einkaufen auch sehr darauf, dass nicht zu viel Plastikverpackung um die Lebensmittel sind. Flaschen werden bei mir sortiert, und was ich überhaupt nicht mag sind Trabis, die Autos, weil sie die Luft verpesten, und darauf könnt ich verzichten.

[**Jutta**] Also, ich versuche auch, also so gut wie's möglich ist, also auch mal zu recyceln, also wir haben bei uns zu Hause, eigentlich nicht zu Hause, also unten im Keller gibt's so 'nen Müllcontainer für verschiedene Sachen, also damit wir das sortieren, so Papier, oder Pappe, oder Flaschen. Und dann mach ich auch das Bestmögliche, dann sortier ich das, und ich finde, man sollte sich schon bemühen, weil wenn alle sich bemühen, dann ist einfach der Müll geringer, und die Natur wird auch nicht so toll belastet. Und na ja, also mit dem Auto, leider fahren meine Eltern beide ein Auto, und na ja, aber ich versuche immer, zu Fuß, oder mit dem Fahrrad zu fahren und, also, ich finde, man muss schon etwas für die Natur tun, weil ... die Natur ist das Wichtigste eigentlich auch.

Kapitel 7 *cont.*

[Silke] Ja, ich fahr auch unheimlich gern Fahrrad, das heißt, wenn es geht, dann fahr ich immer mit dem Fahrrad oder gehe zu Fuß, und wir sind eigentlich kaum mit dem Auto unterwegs. In den Sommerferien habe ich zum Beispiel auch eine Fahrradtour gemacht, weil es hat unheimlichen Spaß gemacht, das Wetter war nur etwas schlecht. Zu Hause, sonst ja was tun wir für die Umwelt? Wir trennen Glas und Altpapier, und es wird jetzt auch eingeführt, dass Kunststoff gesondert gesammelt wird. Zum Beispiel bei meiner Oma wird es schon gesondert gesammelt, ja und sonst denke ich auch, dass alle sich ein bisschen bemühen sollten, die Umwelt noch gut zu erhalten. Das wird dann schon, wenn jeder ein bisschen dazu beiträgt, dann hilft das auch was.

Videoclips: Wetterbericht

Und nun ein Wetterbericht:

Genau, Maxi Biewert und das Wetter für heute, bitte schön.

Ich wünsche Ihnen einen schönen guten Morgen! Und auch heute sieht das Wetter bei uns wieder einige Abwechslung vor. Denn ein Hoch macht sich breit über der Nordsee, aber dazu gleich mehr. Auf dem Satellitenfilm kann ich Ihnen jetzt noch einmal „Johanna" zeigen, das Tief, was uns also gestern beschäftigte, es liegt jetzt hier und verlagert sich weiter nach Südosten. Tja, und für uns ist diese Hochdruckbrücke hier von England bis nach Schweden heute wetterbestimmend, zumindest in der Nordhälfte Deutschlands. Hier wird es nämlich im Tagesverlauf zu Aufheiterungen kommen. Zu Schneefall kommt es allerdings im Süden und Südosten Deutschlands, und dabei bleibt es auch heute. Zu den Temperaturen: 1 Grad plus wird in Leipzig heute erwartet, 3 Grad für München, in Berlin, sowie in Rostock; 4 für Hamburg und in Köln; und Frankfurt an der Spitze mit 5 Grad plus. Zu Schneefall wird es heute auch in Österreich, der Schweiz und Ungarn kommen, aber auch in Prag, Warschau und Oslo gibt es Flockentreiben. In Stockholm gibt es auch Flockentreiben bei 0 Grad, Warschau minus 2 Grad, also hier bleibt die weiße Pracht liegen. Null Grad und richtiges Matschwetter heute für Wien, plus 1 Grad in Zürich; Luxemburg bei 4 Grad, etwas wärmer Palma de Mallorca mit 15 Grad und Sonnenschein, noch wärmer in Athen mit plus 18 Grad, und auch hier scheint heute die Sonne. Zehn Grad für Istanbul, minus 11 Grad für Moskau. In den kommenden drei Tagen ist es nicht mehr ganz so feucht, es kommt also zu Aufheiterungen. Von Nordwesten her greifen sie auf uns über, die Temperaturen verändern sich allerdings kaum.

Videoclips: Werbung

Und wie immer an dieser Stelle: Werbung aus Deutschland

Werbung 1
Jetzt reicht's!

Ich hab euch was mitgebracht! HK-Selbstbausystem, überall passend, unerhört variabel, unverschämt preiswert. HK gibt's nur bei Herte.

Werbung 2
Comics von Siemens — schnell, schnell zum Fachhandel.

Werbung 3
In diesem Haus erlebt gleich jemand sein grünes Wunder: der General mit Bio-Alkohol. Da kommt Glanz ohne Nachwischen, streifenfrei, in einem Wisch. Alles glänzend sauber [*Jingle*: Denn nur was richtig sauber ist ...] Der grüne General mit Bio-Alkohol. [... kann richtig glänzen.]

Werbung 4
Wie sollen diese Flecken bei 40 Grad rausgehen? Wieder nicht raus! Dagegen ist das hier ja richtig grau! Diese drei Probleme haben mit dem Kalk im Wasser zu tun. Deshalb hat Dixan die besonders wirksame Anti-Kalkformel. Dixan beseitigt zuerst den Kalk, dann den Schmutz. Dixan: der Champion unter den Waschmitteln.

Werbung 5
Leiser, sauberer, Alko-Ökostar. Umweltbewusstsein beginnt im eigenen Garten. Alko Spezialist für Gartengeräte.

KAPITEL 8
Einkaufen gehen

Los geht's!

– Hm, Omi, was kochst du denn? Es riecht so gut. Kaiserschmarren? Super!
– Den isst du doch so gern!
– Und wie!

Kapitel 8 *cont.*
– Guten Appetit!
– Und du, Omi, isst du nichts?
– Ich hab schon gegessen. Du weißt doch, ich esse immer um zwölf.
– Ausgezeichnet.
– Freut mich, dass es dir schmeckt.
– Hm, Omi, der Kaiserschmarren war gut! Wie immer!
– Na gut.
– Und? Was soll ich heute für dich einkaufen?
– Hier ist der Einkaufszettel.
– Wo soll ich denn die Tomaten kaufen?
– Die kaufst du im Supermarkt. Dort sind sie nicht so teuer.
– Und das Brot? Kann ich es auch gleich da kaufen?
– Das kaufst du lieber beim Bäcker! Dort ist es immer frisch und schmeckt besser.
– Gut, und was ist mit dem Geld?
– Hier sind hundert Euro. Verlier das Geld nicht!
– Keine Sorge, Omi! Ich pass schon auf!
– Hallo! Grüß dich!
– Grüß Gott!
– Was hättest du ganz gerne?
– Hm, ein Pfund Hackfleisch bitte!
– Hast du sonst noch einen Wunsch, bitte?
– Dann noch hundert Gramm Aufschnitt.
– Sonst noch einen Wunsch außer dem Aufschnitt?
– Nein, danke. Das ist alles.
– Danke schön!
– Danke!
– Grüß Gott!
– Hallo!
– Bitte schön?
– So, ein Brot, bitte!
– Dieses hier?
– Ja, genau das!
– Sonst noch etwas?
– Und dann noch zwei Semmeln.
– Alles dann?
– Danke, das ist alles.
– Macht zwei Euro neunzig, bitte!
– Einen Moment! Dann noch bitte so eine Brezenstange für mich. Nein, die brauchen Sie nicht einpacken, die ess ich gleich.
– Alles dann? 3 Euro 40 dann bitte!
– So, Omi, hier bin ich wieder. Hier sind noch ein Paar Blumen für dich.
– Das ist aber nett!
– So, jetzt packen wir erst mal aus. Die Eier, die Butter. Ja, wo ist denn das Portemonnaie?
– Wo warst du denn zuletzt?
– Einen Moment, Omi, ich bin gleich wieder da! Tschau!

Fortsetzung

– He, Flori, du hast es aber eilig. Geh nie bei Rot über die Straße!
– Was macht ihr denn hier?
– Wir gehen einkaufen. Komm doch mit!
– Da muss ich aber erst meine Omi anrufen!
– Deine Omi?
– Hi, Omi! Was sagst du? Der Geldbeutel ist da? Ja, so ein Glück! Ja, ich komm ein bisschen später. Ist das recht? Okay, gut. Tschau!
– Was ist denn los? Du freust dich ja so!
– Der Geldbeutel ist bei der Oma. Bin ich aber froh!
– Grüß Gott!
– Bitte schön?
– Ein Kilo Tomaten, bitte.
– Sonst noch einen Wunsch?
– Ja, dann brauche ich eine Gurke und einen Salat.
– Sonst noch etwas?
– Die Pfirsiche, die schauen so schön lecker aus.
– Sehr saftig!
– Wie viel Stück brauchen wir denn?
– Sechs Stück.
– Sonst noch etwas?
– Nein, das ist alles.
– Elf achtzig, bitte.
– Danke schön!
– Wiedersehen!
– Wiedersehen!
– So, und was machen wir jetzt?
– Jetzt essen wir erst mal einen Pfirsich.

Landeskunde (in *Pupil's Edition*)

How do you think students in German-speaking countries help others? Here is what some of them said.

Was machst du für andere Leute?

[Silvana] Zweimal in der Woche gebe ich Nachhilfe. Da habe ich einen kleinen Schüler. Der ist in der dritten Klasse, und dem gebe ich eben Nachhilfe in Rechtschreibung und Lesen und Mathematik.

[Sandra] Bei uns in der Nachbarschaft gibt's grad ältere Leute. Und unter uns wohnt 'ne Frau, die ... für die mach ich manchmal kleinere Einkäufe, oder geh einfach nur hin und rede mit ihr, damit sie halt nicht grad so allein ist, oder besuch sie einfach, oder bring ihr halt mal was rüber, wenn wir zum Beispiel Obst aus dem Garten haben. Und ich versuche einfach ein bisschen, so Gesellschaft ihnen, also, bei ihnen zu sein, damit es ihnen nicht so langweilig ist.

Kapitel 8 cont.

[Brigitte] Also, ich hab mit Kindern zu tun. Ich hab mal Kinderkirche sonntags, und da beschäftigt man sich mit kleinen Kindern und spielt mit denen, und das mach ich aber unregelmäßig. Also, ich hab das auch schon eine lange Zeit nicht mehr gemacht.

[Iwan] Also, meistens da helf ich zum Beispiel meinem Bruder irgendwie, wenn er irgendwelche Probleme in der Schule hat. Und wenn ich bei meiner Oma bin, dann helf ich auch meiner Oma.

Videoclips: Werbung

Und wie immer an dieser Stelle: Werbung aus Deutschland

Werbung 1
Neu! Das Nuß-Nougat-Brötchen. Jetzt bei Ihrem Bäcker und Konditor.

Werbung 2
Hast du mein Fruchthäubchen gegessen? Jo, Kurt! Weihenstephan setzt seinen großstückigen Fruchtjoghurts extra eins drauf: ein traumhaft süßes Fruchthäubchen. Wie alles von Weihenstephan. Köstliches aus Milch!

Werbung 3
M wie: Mmm, der ist neu! I wie: Ist der mit Joghurt? L wie: Lecker! R wie: Richtig fruchtig! A wie: Als wär' er selbst gemacht! M wie: Milrams neuer Fruchtquark. Die neue Lust auf Quark und Frucht.

Werbung 4
Gerolsteiner Stille Quelle: Still, mit viel Charakter.

Werbung 5
Also, meine Frau, die macht 'nen Eintopf, hm! Dafür lassen mein Sohn und ich alles andere stehen. Denn da stimmt einfach alles: das frische Gemüse und die Zutaten. Und wenn's mal schnell gehen muss, dann macht sie uns einfach eine leckere Terrine von Sonnen-Bassermann. Sonnen-Bassermann—immer wieder ein Genuss!

Werbung 6
Gutfried-Wurst ist gut für mich, oh yeah! Tutti frutti, Pastete, Mortadella, Salami, Cervelat Gutfried ist gut für mich. Billig und — fit aber voller Geschmack.

Werbung 7
Achten Sie auf Produkte mit dem CMA-Gütezeichen. Kontrollierte Qualität bringt Sicherheit. Wiesenhof-Hähnchen saftig zart, küchenfertig tiefgefroren. Biss für Biss knuspriger Fleischgenuss. Original Wiesenhof. Original „Die Halbrunde" nur von Schulte. Die mustergeschützte Dauerwurst aus gutem Fleisch mit edlen Naturgewürzen. Einmalig! Kaufen Sie kontrollierte Qualität!

KAPITEL 9
Amerikaner in München

Los geht's!

- Die Säfte hier sind doch wirklich Spitze!
- Ja, und vor allem gesund!
- Entschuldigung!
- Ja?
- Wie kommen wir zum Marienplatz?
- Ganz einfach! Immer geradeaus bis zur Ampel und dann nach rechts.
- Das stimmt doch gar nicht! An der Ampel nach links!
- Klar, nach links! Dann kommt ihr direkt zum Marienplatz.
- Ah, vielen Dank.
- Ihr seid Amerikaner, nicht?
- Ja, wir sind aus Wisconsin.
- Wirklich? Was macht ihr hier?
- Ja, wir wohnen in Rosenheim, und heute besuchen wir München.
- Prima! Na dann, viel Spaß!
- Danke schön!
- Tschau!
- Schau! Da kommen die Amerikaner!
- Hallo, Wisconsin, wohin geht's?
- Was esst ihr hier?
- Schau, hier gibt's Bratwurst, Weißwurst, Leberkäs ...
- Der Leberkäs ist hier echt gut.
- Was ist Leber ... Leberkäs?
- Eine bayerische Spezialität. Die musst du mal probieren.
- So, schmeckt's?

Kapitel 9 *cont.*

– Wirklich gut.
– Weißt du was, Markus? Wir zeigen den Amerikanern jetzt die Stadt. Was meint ihr?
– Gute Idee!
– Ich ess jetzt noch fertig, und dann gehen wir.
– Super!

Fortsetzung

– Das ist der Marienplatz, die gute Stube der Münchner.
– Gute Stube, das verstehe ich nicht!
– Gute Stube ist das Wohnzimmer zu Hause, und hier auf dem Marienplatz fühlen sich die Leute wie zu Hause. Du kannst hier lesen, essen, miteinander sprechen, und du kannst hier viel Musik hören.
– Jetzt versteh ich die gute Stube.
– Das ist das Münchner Kindl, das Wahrzeichen der Stadt, und dort oben ist das Glockenspiel. Kommt, wir gehen jetzt rechts um die Ecke zum Dom! Das ist der Dom. Er hat zwei Türme. Hier sind wir in der Fußgängerzone. Der Strauss-Brunnen. Hübsch, nicht? Der ... Vorsicht, da kommt eine Strassenbahn! Das berühmte Hofbräuhaus. Vor uns das Nationaltheater. Wenn ihr eine Oper hören wollt, müsst ihr hierher kommen. Die Residenz. Hier haben die Könige von Bayern gewohnt. Vor uns die Feldherrnhalle, wie die Loggia in Florenz. Die Theatinerkirche, Barockstil. Und das ist der Hofgarten, eine Oase in der Stadt. Wie gefallen euch die schönen Blumen?
– Sehr schön!
– Aber es ist so schön spät. Wir müssen zurück nach Rosenheim!
– Schade!
– Wo kriegen wir den Zug?
– Am Bahnhof natürlich.
– Und wie kommen wir am besten zum Bahnhof?
– Am besten mit der U-Bahn. Sie ist gleich da draußen.
– Habt ihr U-Bahnkarten?
– Nein.
– Hier ist 'ne Streifenkarte. So zweimal umknicken, und so geht's.
– Ja, danke.
– So, auf Wiederschau'n! Vielleicht sehen wir uns ja mal in Amerika.
– Ja, bestimmt!
– Und vielen Dank!
– Tschüs!

Landeskunde (in *Pupil's Edition*)

We asked some people in the German-speaking countries to tell us about what kind of foods they like to eat. Guess what most of them told us.

Was isst du gern?

[Melina] Okay, ich esse am liebsten so Eis, vor allem Erdbeereis oder so, mit Früchten drin. Und so von Gerichten mag ich ja Schnitzel oder Linseneintopf. Ja, trinken mag ich ... mag ich eigentlich so mehr Cola oder so Apfelsaft.

[Rosi] Also, gerne esse ich Gulasch, aber nur von meiner Oma, wenn die das macht. Und sonst, also was ich überhaupt nicht esse ist Paprika, aber warum ich das nicht esse, kann ich nicht sagen, schmeckt mir einfach nicht. Sonst esse ich gerne, ach, ich esse oft gern Süßspeisen, also Kaiserschmarren, das ist österreichisch, oder Eierkuchen, ja. Also eigentlich alles Mögliche.

[Uli] Also, ungerne Pizza, die Freunde von mir auch. Was esse ich gerne? Ziemlich viel Gemüse, frisch gekocht. Also, ich mag es nicht, ständig in Restaurants zu gehen und dort zu essen. Ich hab selten Hunger, aber dafür manchmal richtig groß auf Fastfood, sprich weg McDonald's®, was ja auch die amerikanischen Studenten sicherlich gut kennen werden. Aber das kommt nur so alle zwei Monate mal vor. Dafür liebe ich Würstchen jeglicher Art, besonders so die Berliner Currywürstchen, die es hier in München leider nicht so oft gibt. Ja, und das ist so das, was ich gerne esse. Und es ist mehr die italienische Küche, weniger die deutsche.

Landeskunde (on Video only)

[Kali] Hamburger, Cheeseburger ...

[Uli] Entweder Tortellini oder Ravioli.

[Berta] Viel Spaghetti.

[Philipp] Also, zu essen, üblich ist ja halt Fleisch, grad McDonald's oder so, wenn man schnell was essen möchte. Sonst das Übliche, Landspezialitäten, Wurst mit Spätzle, ja so was halt. Kein Gemüse.

[Martin] Also, ich mag halt hauptsächlich chinesisch, japanisch und so, das ist, das esse ich halt, da mag ich halt asiatisch, das ist mein Lieblingsessen.

[Susanne] Am liebsten esse ich italienisch, ja weil es mir am besten schmeckt.

Kapitel 9 *cont.*

[**Martina**] Ich esse keinen Fisch, beziehungsweise gar nichts, was aus dem Meer kommt. Keine Ahnung warum, also ich mochte es noch nie, weiß nicht.

[**Frau Troger**] Gulasch mit Semmelknödeln und Salat. Oder Knödel oder Speckknödel, Kasnocken, weiß nicht, ob Sie das kennen ...

[**Brigitte**] Also im Moment sehr im Schwabenland hier, und da würde ich sagen also, was typisch wär' zum Beispiel, Spätzle heißt das, und das heißt ja von Deutschland so Sauerkraut, aber ich würde das eigentlich weniger sagen. Vielleicht so Knödel noch, oder so was in die Richtung.

[**Trudi**] Ja, also ich esse alles, und gerne esse ich eigentlich Lasagne.

[**Marta**] Also, ganz gern essen tu ich Spaghetti und Pizza und Salat, und rote Beete mag ich überhaupt nicht.

[**Helmut**] Also Pizza, Spätzle und so esse ich gern. Spinat also nicht so.

[**Johannes**] Also, am liebsten esse ich Pizza, und was ich nicht gern esse, ist eigentlich Spaghetti.

[**Helene**] Also gut, ich esse eigentlich alles ziemlich gern, aber am liebsten Fastfood, das schmeckt immer noch am besten. Und zu Hause halt meistens griechisches Essen, aber auch deutsches, eigentlich ist alles gemischt. Es ist alles vorhanden, was ich am liebsten mag. Und was ich eigentlich nicht gerne esse — Spinat muss nicht unbedingt sein.

[**Marga**] Also ich esse eigentlich ziemlich alles gern und auch vor allem italienische Spezialitäten wie Pizza oder Lasagne, oder auch chinesische Sachen. Ja, und daheim kochen wir vorwiegend deutsch, aber auch italienisch oder auch indonesisch mal, je nachdem, wie wir es gern wollen.

[**Heinz**] Ich esse keinen Fisch. Sonst esse ich Rouladen mit Klößen am liebsten.

[**Eva**] Ja, ich probiere eigentlich alles. Spätzle nicht so gern, aber ansonsten alles.

[**Elke**] Ich liebe es, im Urlaub nach Italien zu fahren, und deshalb esse ich sehr gerne Pizza und koche sehr gerne Spaghettis und ja, deutsche Kost, vielleicht noch Kohlrouladen.

[**Ria**] Also, ich esse unheimlich gerne Salat, und Spaghetti, jede Woche bestimmt dreimal esse ich das auch.

[**Jens**] Also, ich esse auch gern italienische Sachen, so wie Spaghetti, Pizza, und Außereuropäisches mag ich auch, chinesisch oder spanisch, mexikanisch, und eben frische Sachen ess ich auch sehr gerne.

[**Jasmin**] Ich esse gerne Spaghetti, und Mohrrüben hasse ich, also Mohrrüben esse ich überhaupt nicht gerne.

[**Stefan**] Sehr verschieden gerne. Also erst mal deutsche Küche, aber ich geh auch gerne ausländisch essen. Hier gibt es viele China-Restaurants oder türkische Restaurants. Griechische in Berlin gibt es sehr viele, und ich geh gern abwechslungsreich essen.

[**Ingo**] Pommes, Hamburger, Currywurst, ja.

Videoclips: Werbung

Und wie immer an dieser Stelle: Werbung aus Deutschland

Werbung 1
Das Siemens-Museum München. Prannerstraße 10. Geöffnet Montag bis Freitag von 9 bis 16 Uhr. Samstag und Sonntag 10 bis 14 Uhr. Normalerweise.

Werbung 2
Nordsee. Meer erleben.

Werbung 3
Hier sehen Sie Klaus-Peter W. bei seinen Bankgeschäften. Postbank: die clevere Alternative.

Werbung 4
Hier sehen Sie Klaus-Peter W. auf dem Weg zu seiner Bank. Postbank: die clevere Alternative.

LOCATION OPENER: Baden-Württemberg

Hallo, und herzlich willkommen in Baden-Württemberg und in der Stadt Bietigheim. Ich heiße Sabine Junius, bin 15 Jahre alt, gehe hier aufs Ellental-Gymnasium. Bietigheim liegt in einer schönen Gegend, 25 Kilometer nordwestlich von Stuttgart. Wollt ihr unsere schöne Gegend und die Stadt Bietigheim kennen lernen? Ich führe euch gerne herum. Also los, kommt mit!

Baden-Württemberg — ein grünes Land, mit vielen alten Burgen und Schlössern.

Hier Monrepos, in der Nähe von Ludwigsburg.

Kleine, mittelalterliche Städte wie Besigheim, von grünen Weinbergen umgeben.

Vom Stadtpark in Bietigheim aus hat man einen tollen Blick auf meine Heimatstadt Bietigheim.

Die Hauptstraße, jetzt Fußgängerzone, mit dem schönen mittelalterlichen Stadttor.

Die Evangelische Stadtkirche, erbaut in den Jahren 1401 bis 1411.

Das Kleine Bürgerhaus, ein Fachwerkhaus aus dem 17. Jahrhundert.

Das Bietigheimer Schloss aus dem Jahre 1380.

Das Rathaus ist ein prachtvoller Bau. Jeden Samstag ist hier Markttag auf dem Rathausplatz.

Und wir haben eine ganz schmale, lustige Gasse: unser Hexenwegle.

Hallo, da bin ich wieder. Und das sind meine Freunde und Klassenkameraden. Ihr werdet uns gleich noch ganz gut kennen lernen. Also bis gleich, und tschüs!

Tschüs!

KAPITEL 10
Kino und Konzerte

Los geht's!

– Ah, was für schöne Blumen, diese Farben, einfach prächtig. Aber schau! Unsere Jugend. Da sitzen sie und tun überhaupt nichts. Sie sollten zu Hause sein und ihre Hausaufgaben machen. Das sind doch richtige Faulenzer. Aber du siehst: sie tun nichts, überhaupt nichts!
– Was, nichts?
– Hier, wir joggen! Hier, wir kegeln! Hier, wir radeln! Hier, wir segeln! Und wir singen, fahren Skateboard, spielen Karten, und wir helfen alten Leuten!
– Faulenzer sind wir nicht!
– Hier, wir lesen, diskutieren, spielen Schach, musizieren, und wir lachen, spielen Karten, und sind traurig, ja sehr traurig, müssen warten!
– Mensch, wo sind die anderen nur?
– Sabine ist bestimmt noch zu Hause und liest.
– Du hast Recht, ich lese furchtbar gerne. Schau mal, wie viele Bücher ich habe. Ich lese gerade dieses Buch, das ist absolute Spitze.
– So was, in zehn Minuten beginnt der Film.
– Die Sandra, die holt doch den Martin ab. Vielleicht schauen sie sich ja Musikkassetten an.
– Schau Martin, Country Western, nichts für dich?
– Du weißt doch, ich mag die meisten Countrysänger nicht. Da, das ist was für mich. Ein Konzertabend mit Schülern der Musikschule: Brahms, Ravel. Der Eintritt ist frei.
– Ja, schau, da kommt ja der Thomas. Hi!
– Tag!
– Du, lass mich mal hören! Klasse Rock, prima!
– Das sind die „Toten Hosen". Die hör ich am liebsten.
– Hallo, wir sind da!
– Tag!
– Ich auch. Hallo! Wartet ihr schon lange?
– Nein, gar nicht. Nur eine Viertelstunde.
– Was läuft denn heute?
– Action oder Fantasy.
– Also ich seh am liebsten Fantasyfilme.
– Ich nicht.
– Ich bin für Action.
– Ich auch. Also rein ins Kino.
– Mensch, du spinnst doch! Ihr könnt alleine gehen, ich hasse Actionfilme.
– Kinder, Kinder! Wir können nicht lange diskutieren, der Film beginnt in wenigen Minuten.

Fortsetzung

– Ich fand den Film nicht gut. Und ihr?
– Ich mag solche Filme nicht.
– Ich fand ihn langweilig.
– Er war viel zu lang.
– Komm, lass uns nach Hause gehen und ein Video anschauen.

Kapitel 10 *cont.*

MUSIKVIDEO: Die Prinzen: Ich wär so gerne Millionär

Ich wär so gerne Millionär,

Dann wär' mein Konto niemals leer.

Ich wär so gerne Millionär, millionenschwer!

Ich wär so gerne Millionär, Geld, Geld, Geld,

Ich hab kein Geld, hab keine Ahnung, doch ich hab ein großes Maul. Weder Doktor noch Professor, aber ich bin stinkend faul.

Ich habe keine reiche Freundin, und keinen reichen Freund,

Von viel Kohle hab ich bisher leider nur geträumt.

Was soll ich tun, was soll ich machen?

Bin vor Kummer schon halb krank. Hab mir schon 'n paar Mal überlegt, vielleicht knackst du eine Bank. Doch das ist leider sehr gefährlich, bestimmt werd ich gefasst. Und außerdem bin ich doch ehrlich, und will nicht in den Knast.

Ich wär so gerne Millionär, dann wär' mein Konto niemals leer. Ich wär so gerne Millionär, millionenschwer! Ich wär so gerne Millionär.

Es gibt so viele reiche Witwen, die begehr'n mich sehr. Sie sind so scharf auf meinen Körper, doch den geb ich nicht her. Ich kann das wirklich nicht verkraften, um keinen Preis der Welt, deswegen werd ich lieber Popstar und schwimm in meinem Geld.

Ich wär so gerne Millionär, dann wär' mein Konto niemals leer. Ich wär so gerne Millionär, millionenschwer! Ich wär so gerne Millionär.

Ich wär so gerne Millionär, dann wär' mein Konto niemals leer. Ich wär so gerne Millionär, millionenschwer! Ich wär so gerne Millionär.

Ich wär so gerne Millionär, dann wär' mein Konto niemals leer. Ich wär so gerne Millionär, millionenschwer! Ich wär so gerne Millionär.

Millionär!

Landeskunde (in *Pupil's Edition*)

We asked several teenagers what cultural events they usually go to for entertainment. What do you think they said?

Welche kulturellen Veranstaltungen besuchst du?

[Silvana] Also, kulturelle Veranstaltungen — geh ich manchmal ins Ballett mit meiner Mutter, also uns interessiert das Ballett: *Schwanensee* war ich schon, *Nussknacker* von Tschaikowsky, und ab und zu gehen wir mit der Schule ins Museum oder zu irgendwelchen Ausstellungen, aber eigentlich nicht sehr oft.

[Tim] Also, ich versuch's so oft wie möglich, bei jeder Chance, in ein Theater oder in eine Oper zu gehen, sobald ich günstig Karten bekomme, das heißt über die Schule krieg ich Vergünstigung, oder dass meine Eltern mich halt einladen oder was sponsern, dass ich dann ins Theater gehe. Und es wird auch sehr oft im Klassenunterricht halt so was angeboten, dass man darüber 'ne Klausur schreibt. Da geh ich halt jedes Mal mit.

[Silke] Ich geh auch gern ins Theater, ich kuck mir auch mal Shakespeare an oder so, und auch mal so witzige Theaterstücke, und ich geh auch sehr gern ins Museum. Und es gab da hier vor kurzem die Picasso-Ausstellung, und die war eigentlich auch ganz gut.

[Rosi] Also, ich geh nicht oft zu kulturellen Veranstaltungen, weil meine Eltern wollen mich zwar mal mitnehmen, aber ich hab dann andere Sachen vor, dann bin verabredet und hab keine Lust. Aber meine Eltern sind schon dafür, dass ich da hingehen würde.

Landeskunde (on Video only)

[Susanne] Ich gehe gern ins Kino, gehe gern ins Theater, lese sehr viel.

[Martina] Gut, also wenn man Kino als kulturell bezeichnen kann, dann Kino, ich lese viel und mag Museen sehr gerne. Ansonsten ist die Freizeit sehr knapp, also wenn sich's einrichten lässt, immer.

[Ilse] Ja, also wenn man sich wirklich sehr für Kultur interessiert, kann man einmal hier in Wedel zwar ins Kino gehen, und ein kleines Theater gibt es hier auch, ab und zu wird auch was draußen aufgeführt so auf der Leinwand, aber man kann eben auch nach Hamburg fahren, wo man selbstverständlich viel mehr Auswahl hat.

[Andreas] Ja, wir haben uns hier jetzt *Cats* angeguckt, und *Phantom der Oper* war leider ausverkauft. So Musicals sind halt sehr schön. Am liebsten hätt ich sie im Original gesehen, weil ... den Text versteht man eh nicht so richtig, im Deutschen selbst, and da ist mir im

Kapitel 10 *cont.*

Englischen oder Amerikanischen—es ist mir halt lieber, die anzusehen, als jetzt hier ... na ja, die *Cats* ... ich weiß nicht ... war nicht so schön ... im Original stell ich mir's schöner vor.

[Monika] Ich gehe gerne in Museum und Ausstellungen über berühmte Maler und Dichter, so was alles mach ich gern.

[Hans] Ja, manchmal geh ich ins Theater ... ja, mehr wird hier auch nicht geboten, an kulturellen Veranstaltungen ... Theater.

[Julia] Wenn mir Zeit dazu bleibt, ins Theater, oder jetzt momentan ist ja Picasso-Ausstellung hier in Hamburg, da geh ich auch noch hin ... meistens Theater.

[Jutta] Also, ich geh ziemlich gern ins Theater. Es gibt auch Angebote für Jugendliche, einen Theaterpass zum Beispiel. Da kriegt man ja ziemlich Vergünstigungen, um ins Theater zu gehen, um mal in die Oper zu gehen, aber auch Musikveranstaltungen, wenn zum Beispiel irgendwelche Bands spielen, was dann auch teilweise kulturell ist ... zum Beispiel aus Jamaika, irgendwelche Informationabende oder so.

Videoclips: Werbung

Und wie immer an dieser Stelle, Werbung aus Deutschland!

Werbung 1
Jetzt in Ihrer Videothek: *Die unendliche Geschichte 2*. Ein phantastisches Abenteuer, das Millionen begeisterte. *Die unendliche Geschichte 2*, denn Video bringt Kinohits zuerst auf den Bildschirm. Warum warten?

Werbung 2
Gute Zeiten-Schlechte Zeiten. Für alle Fans jetzt das Album zur RTL-Fernsehserie. Und was meint ihr dazu? Super! Klar! *Gute Zeiten-Schlechte Zeiten*. Unsere Superhits zur Serie. Jetzt neu!

Werbung 3
RTL präsentiert: Andreas Elsholz und seine neue Single *Gib mir noch Zeit*. In jeder CD-Single steckt ein Original-Autogramm. Die neue Single von Andreas Elsholz, dem Heiko Richter aus *Gute Zeiten-Schlechte Zeiten*. Jetzt brandneu!

Werbung 4
Sie ist endlich fertig geworden. Und sie ist gut. Sehr gut sogar, glaube ich. Howard Carpendale. Ganz nah. So nah wie noch nie.

Werbung 5
Vergesst alles andere. Jetzt neu! Bravo Hits 4. Alle euere Superhits. Mit dem original Nummer-Eins-Hit von *Snow*. Bravo Hits 4 —Holt euch euere Nummer Eins!

Werbung 6
NDR 2 präsentiert: Das Drei-Tage Open Air Festival in Lüneburg vom 3. bis 5. September. Mit Prince — Chris de Burgh — Rod Stewart — Tina Turner und vielen anderen Superstars. Eintrittskarten bei allen Vorverkaufsstellen und an der Tageskasse.

Werbung 7
Knackfrisch — das muss ein Leibniz sein. Leibniz Butterkeks — knackfrisch. Nur echt mit 52 Zähnen.

Werbung 8
Tagtäglich passieren Dinge auf dieser Welt, für die es scheinbar keine Erklärung gibt. Sie widersprechen physikalischen Gesetzen, entziehen sich jeglicher Logik und werfen unlösbare Fragen auf. *Rätselhafte Phänomene.* Ab sofort zeigt ein neues Sammelwerk Woche für Woche die fesselndsten Geheimnisse unseres Universums. Berichte, Beweise, Theorien. *Rätselhafte Phänomene.* Die Welt des Unerklärlichen. Jetzt bei ihrem Zeitschriftenhändler.

KAPITEL 11
Der Geburtstag

Los geht's!

– Kroll!
– Guten Tag, Frau Kroll! Hier ist die Nicole. Ist die Sabine da?
– Nein. Sabine ist mit ihrem Vater weg. Kann ich ihr etwas sagen?
– Ja, hm ... sagen Sie ihr bitte, dass der Martin am Samstag Geburtstag hat. Und ich möchte für ihn eine Fete organisieren.
– Na, prima! Ich sag es Sabine. Tschüs!
– Wiederhören, Frau Kroll!
– Was schenkst du dem Martin?
– Kein Problem! Ich kaufe ihm eine Kassette.
– Aber er hat doch schon so viele Kassetten.
– Na und?
– Warum kaufst du ihm keine CD?
– Er hat doch noch keinen CD-Player.

Kapitel 11 cont.

- Was soll ich ihm bloß schenken? Was meinst du? Du kennst ihn besser. Eine Idee?
- Kauf ihm doch ein Buch. Er liest auch gerne.
- Bücher sind so teuer.
- Dann schenk ihm halt ein T-Shirt. Mit einem Komponisten drauf. Das mag er bestimmt auch.
- Eine prima Idee!
- Schau mal, Nicole! Die Karte ist lustig, nicht?
- Wahnsinn! Und lies mal den Vers!
- Die schenk ich dem Martin!

Fortsetzung

- Übrigens, weißt du, wann der Thomas Geburtstag hat?
- Irgendwann im Sommer. Ich glaub im August.
- An welchem Tag?
- Warum fragst du? Willst du ... ?
- Nein, nein. Seinen Geburtstag feiern wir nie.
- Im August haben wir immer Ferien.
- Zeig her!
- Schau, hier: am elften August.
- Hier steht: Martin am achtzehnten. Er hat also nicht diesen Samstag Geburtstag.
- Was? Das kann doch nicht wahr sein! Was soll ich jetzt machen? Die kommen alle diesen Samstag!

Landeskunde (in *Pupil's Edition*)

We asked several teenagers what they usually give as birthday presents. Here is what some of them said.

Was schenkst du zum Geburtstag?

[Melanie] Meinen Geburtstag feier ich an sich gar nicht weiter. Ich geh mit Freunden essen oder lade sie zu mir ein. Und dann sitzen wir zusammen und unterhalten uns nett oder Ähnliches. Ansonsten gar nicht weiter. Und bei Familienmitgliedern ist es ähnlich, da feiern wir auch in der Familie. Und schenken tu ich dann meiner Schwester zum Beispiel, die hört ziemlich gerne Musik, und der schenk ich dann Kassetten oder CDs oder Ähnliches. Und ansonsten eben schenke ich Bücher oder eben andere Kleinigkeiten, für die sich die Freunde oder Familienmitglieder interessieren.

[Eva] Eigentlich hass ich Geburtstage, weil ich nie weiß, was ich schenken soll. Es ist irgendwie immer dasselbe, Bücher oder Kassetten oder CDs. Und na ja, dann sucht man sich immer was aus. Meistens verschenkt man Gutscheine, weil—dann kann man nichts falsch machen. Na ja.

[Rosi] Also, wenn ich auf Geburtstage gehe von Freunden oder Freundinnen, die ich gut kenne, dann geb ich auch mal mehr Geld aus. Dann kriegen sie schon persönliche Geschenke, wo sie sich auch darüber freuen. Und wenn ich auf Geburtstage gehe von Leuten, die ich nicht so gut kenne, dann nehme ich nur Kleinigkeiten mit. Aber ich nehm eigentlich immer was mit, wenn ich auf Geburtstage gehe.

[Jutta] Ich hab einen kleinen Bruder, und der ist elf, und der spielt unheimlich gern mit Lego® ... und dem schenk ich dann was zum Spielen oder eine Musikkassette. Und wenn ich bei Freunden eingeladen bin, meistens Selbstgemachtes, ein bemaltes T-Shirt, ja auch eine Musikkassette, ein Buch oder ein gemaltes Bild.

Landeskunde (on Video only)

[Jürgen] Wenn ich meinen Geburtstag feiere, dann lad ich ziemlich viele Freunde ein, dann machen wir eine Art kleine Disko ... und, ja ... stehen zusammen, unterhalten uns, feiern. Dazu essen wir meistens einfache Sachen, Salate, vielleicht mal eine Pizza, so was in der Richtung.

[Eva] Ja, also wenn's ein Geburtstag ist, da nehm ich ein Geschenk mit, ansonsten also 'ne Flasche Sekt.

[Bianca] Ein Geschenk ... und Musikkassetten, CDs, vielleicht ein paar Spiele oder so.

[Helmut] Ja, das kommt auf ihn selber an, CDs oder so, Bücher, was er braucht.

[Roland] Also, erst einmal mit meiner Familie gehen wir essen, dann ein, zwei Tage später lade ich ein paar Freunde ein, miete vielleicht einen Raum, oder ich geh mit denen Billiard spielen oder ins Kino.

[Jochen] Ja, bei uns auch ist erst Familientag angesagt, also Verwandte, Tanten, Kusinen einladen und dann essen gehen und zu Hause selber was machen ... und dann, wie gesagt, zwei, drei Tage später mit Freunden irgendwas machen, 'ne Party machen oder Kegeln gehen, Billiard spielen gehen und so.

[Annika] Ja, das kommt auf die Person drauf an. Manchmal back ich 'nen Kuchen, oder, halt ... kommt drauf an, was der sich auch wünscht.

Kapitel 11 *cont.*

Wenn er sagt: ich möchte die und die CD haben, dann schenk ich die ihm auch.

[Fabian] Ja, es kommt eigentlich auf die Person an. Also meistens überlegen wir uns mit zwei oder drei noch Freunden irgendeinen ausgefallenen, ausgeflippten Wunsch, den er hat, und den erfüllen wir dann, oder Gutscheine für irgendwelche CDs, oder 'nen Abend mal mit uns, oder so. Aber hauptsächlich irgendwelche ausgeflippten Sachen.

[Silke] Na, ich hab auch drei Geschwister noch, die sind alle kleiner als ich, und wenn sie Geburtstag haben, dann schenk ich auch eher so Spielzeugsachen, zum Beispiel der eine mag Playmobil™, schenk ich ihm Playmobil™ — na ja, und wenn ich zu Freunden gehe, dann ist es ja eigentlich Tradition, dass man ihnen eigentlich so witzige Sachen eher schenkt, so von uns selbst ausgedacht und so, meistens ein beliebtes T-Shirt mit einer witzigen Karikatur oder so.

Videoclips: Werbung

Und wie immer an dieser Stelle, Werbung aus Deutschland!

Werbung 1
Du, ich kaufe 'nen Schoko-Weihnachtsmann für die Kinder. So einen, nicht? Wieso? Weihnachtsmann ist Weihnachtsmann, äußerlich vielleicht. Schau mal: Milka hat die Auswahl, die Kindern schmeckt. Sogar weiße Schokolade und Nuss. Oh, Milka! Weiße Schokolade! Ich hab Nuss! Und Oma freut sich über ihr geliebtes „I love Milka" Nuß-Nougat. Für wen mögen wohl die Neuen sein: „I love Milka" Schokola-Sahne, Nuß-Japonais, und Edelmarzipan? Jetzt in vier Sorten. Milka — die zarteste Versuchung, seit es Schokolade gibt.

Werbung 2
Du bist der hellste Punkt an meinem Horizont. Du bist der Farbenklecks in meinem Grau in Grau. Du bist in meiner Winterzeit der Sonnenstrahl. Merci, dass es dich gibt. Du bist die Wasserflut für meinen Wüstensand. Du bist der Fels, der in meiner Brandung steht. Du bist in meinem Lieblingslied die Melodie. Merci, dass es dich gibt.

Werbung 3
Diese Telefonnummer bitte gleich notieren. Es lohnt sich! Guten Tag! Heute haben Sie die einmalige Gelegenheit, die neue Brockhaus-Enzyklopädie kennen zu lernen, denn Brockhaus ist wichtig für den Erfolg in der Schule, im Studium, im Beruf, und für das ganze Leben. Zum Kennenlernen haben wir zwei Geschenke für Sie: Geschenk 1: diese wertvolle Informationsbroschüre mit vielen Originalseiten aus der neuen Brockhaus-Enzyklopädie. Geschenk 2: diese plastische Großpanoramakarte, die Ihnen ganz Deutschland in all seinen Details zeigt. Beide Geschenke können Sie jetzt zum Nulltarif anfordern. Exklusiv vom renommierten Weltbild-Verlag. Wählen Sie bitte 0130-5251. Wir freuen uns auf Ihren Anruf!

KAPITEL 12
Die Fete
(Wiederholungskapitel)

Los geht's!

– Hallo!
– Hallo!
– Du bist aber pünktlich!
– Wie immer.
– Das Rad, das stellst du am besten an die Wand. Da kommt auch schon der Andreas! Hallo!
– Tag, Nicole! Tag, Thomas!
– Tag!
– So, Nicole, was können wir für dich tun?
– Zuerst muss ich einkaufen gehen. Wer will mitkommen? Ich muss zum Supermarkt.
– Wir beide können ja mit den Rädern fahren.
– Lieb von dir! Aber wir müssen ja so viel einkaufen. Die Mutti fährt uns mit dem Auto hin. Aber du kannst mitkommen, wenn du willst.
– Klar!
– Und was mache ich?
– Thomas, du kannst dem Vati im Garten helfen, und dann müssen wir noch das Gemüse waschen.
– Okay! Wir können das ja machen, wenn wir zurückkommen.
– Hallo!
– Da seid ihr ja schon. Schaut, ich bin auch fleißig. Ich wasche das Gemüse.
– Na prima, Vati. Wo ist denn der Thomas?
– Der will den Rasen mähen. Der braucht mich nicht. Was habt ihr mitgebracht? Bratwurst.
– Oh, die Bratwurst sieht gut aus. Hm, ganz frisch! Und was habt ihr sonst noch?

Kapitel 12 cont.

- Wir haben noch Eier, Mehl, Zucker. Andreas und ich, wir backen dann einen Kuchen.
- Schön.
- Was brauchen wir denn alles?
- Ein halbes Pfund Butter, 200 Gramm Zucker, 4 Eier und 400 Gramm Mehl. Ach ja, und das Backpulver dürfen wir nicht vergessen.
- So viel?
- Klar! Und jetzt hinein damit in den Ofen. Ungefähr 200 Grad, da kann nichts passieren.
- Thomas, der Rasen sieht toll aus! Du kannst gut mähen.
- Du, sag mir mal, was soll ich denn mit dem Gras hier tun? In die Mülltonne geben?
- Mensch, du spinnst wohl! Das Gras kommt auf den Komposthaufen, dort hinten in der Ecke. Wir sind doch hier sehr umweltfreundlich.
- Entschuldigung! Du, kannst du mir jetzt helfen, die Flaschen zur Mülltonne zu bringen?
- Also, rein mit den Flaschen!
- Halt, die Flaschen kommen in die grüne Tonne!
- Mensch, mein Kuchen!
- Mutti! Mein Kuchen! Ach, du meine Güte! Schau mal, mein Kuchen! Sieht er nicht toll aus? Was machen wir jetzt?

Fortsetzung

- Hallo, da seid ihr ja!
- Hallo!
- Hallo!
- Kommt mit auf die Terrasse!
- Die Geschenke, Nicole?
- Die kommen ins Wohnzimmer.
- Nimm mein Geschenk doch auch gleich mit.
- Mach ich.
- Hallo Sabine!
- Hallo! Tolle Schürze!
- Oh ja, die wird bald schmutzig sein. Da kommt ja der Andreas!
- Guten Tag!
- Hallo!
- Hallihallo Sabine! Siehst echt fesch aus. Gefällt mir wirklich.
- Wirklich?
- Wirklich!
- Was wollt ihr trinken?
- Ist das Erdbeerbowle?
- Ja.
- Ja, bitte.
- Ein Glas Erdbeerbowle.
- Danke!
- Und für mich bitte ein Glas Orangensaft.
- Ein Glas Orangensaft.
- Danke sehr!

- Ein Glas Limo für mich, bitte.
- Danke! Wann kommt denn der Martin?
- Um Viertel vor vier, wenn alle da sind.
- Habt ihr hier denn keine Musik?
- Doch, was wollt ihr denn hören?
- Rock für mich.
- Du und dein Rock. Ich leg eine CD auf, meine Lieblings-CD. Etwas für alle, ja?
- Wie du meinst, okay, okay.
- Hallo, Martin! Hallo, Sandra!
- Hallo! Kommen wir zu spät?
- Nein, überhaupt nicht, es fehlen noch welche. Vati, das ist Martin.
- Hallo Martin! Herzlich willkommen bei uns!
- Guten Tag! Vielen Dank für die Einladung.
- Schon gut! Wir freuen uns, wenn wir einmal im Jahr Nicoles Freunde zu uns einladen können. Was willst du trinken? — Andreas, willst du Martin etwas zu trinken geben? Ich muss zum Grill.
- Okay Martin, was möchtest du denn haben?
- Die Bowle schmeckt gut.
- Gut, dann probier ich die Bowle!
- Hier bitte!
- Prost!
- Hm, die ist wirklich gut.
- So, Kinder, das Essen ist fertig. Fangt dort drüben an und kommt dann hier herüber.
- So, wer möchte was? Es gibt Kartoffelsalat, Krautsalat, Gurkensalat, Tomatensalat. Thomas, möchtest du Kartoffelsalat?
- Ja, bitte! Die Wurstbrote sehen auch ganz lecker aus.
- Nimm doch gleich zwei, und eine Brezel!
- Okay! Wo ist denn der Kuchen?
- Pst, der Kuchen kommt gleich nachher.
- Ach so!
- Herzlichen Glückwunsch, Martin!
- Happy Birthday to you! Happy Birthday to you! Happy Birthday, dear Martin! Happy Birthday to you!
- Was für eine Überraschung! Vielen, vielen Dank!
- Herzlichen Glückwunsch zum Geburtstag, Martin!
- Danke, Nicole!

Landeskunde (in *Pupil's Edition*)

You've already discovered how German students like to spend their free time, and you know that they enjoy planning and going to parties. However, life isn't all fun! Often, before they go out and meet with their friends, they have to help around the house. What chores do you think German students have to do? Here is what some of them told us.

Kapitel 12 cont.
Musst du zu Hause helfen?

[Heide] Und ich muss zweimal in der Woche die Toilette sauber machen, und dann ab und zu halt den Geschirrspüler ausräumen oder die Küche wischen und halt mein Zimmer aufräumen.

[Silvana] Zu Hause helf ich meistens so beim Abwaschen, Spülmaschine ausräumen, oder die Wäsche aufhängen oder abnehmen, zusammenlegen, immer so, was anfällt. Ist meistens irgendwas am Tag. Und ich hab noch 'nen Bruder, der hilft dann auch immer mit und ja, das war's.

[Monika] Also, ich muss fast jeden Tag den Mülleimer runterbringen und ab und zu mal Waschmaschine an, Waschmaschine aus, Wäsche aufhängen und, wenn sie trocken ist, abnehmen und zusammenlegen. Dann ab und zu Staub saugen, wischen—also wir haben in der Küche so Fliesen und im Bad auch, manchmal wischen, aber meistens, wenn meine Eltern keine Zeit dazu haben. Abwaschen muss ich nicht, also wir haben einen Geschirrspüler.

[Gerd] Ich saug halt ab und zu Staub und räum Spülmaschine aus, bring Müll raus, hol halt teilweise Getränke und so, mäh manchmal den Rasen—kommt ganz darauf an.

Landeskunde (on Video only)

[Trude] Ja, ich muss halt mein Zimmer sauber machen, und dann halt öfters putzen halt. Mal kochen, wenn meine Mutter nicht da ist.

[Maren] Mein Zimmer aufräumen, so in der Küche mithelfen, und Tisch abräumen.

[Helmut] Ja, ab und zu abtrocknen, spülen halt ab und zu.

[Johannes] Zu Hause tu ich ja, wenn ich was mach, dann Rasen mähen.

[Marco] Ja, ich muss Rasen mähen, und ab und zu mal Geschirr abwaschen und Staub saugen.

[Ulla] Also, ich helf zu Hause relativ wenig mit, und wenn, dann muss ich abwaschen oder Treppe putzen. Und ich bin für den Garten verantwortlich, das heißt also Rosen schneiden oder Blumen pflanzen. Und ich hab ein Haustier, einen Hamster, und den muss ich auch versorgen.

[Heidemarie] Also, ich helfe ab und zu mal in der Küche oder im Garten, hab leider keine Haustiere, um die ich mich kümmern muss, aber ich helf auch ab und zu in der Kehrwoche mit und mach irgendwo ab und zu mal was.

[Marga] Ja, also ich muss zu Hause schon etwas machen, gut, nicht so viel, aber zum Beispiel Wäsche bügeln, abtrocknen, Geschirr spülen, abstauben und saugen, das gehört natürlich schon dazu, und ich mein, ich mach das auch gerne. Weil wir haben ein großes Haus, und da geht natürlich nicht alles immer alleine ... Ich kann das auch nicht immer von meinen Eltern, speziell von meiner Mutter oder so, erwarten, und das geht ganz gut auch.

[Alexandra] Ja, ich muss auch oft bügeln, oder mal Bad und Küche putzen und Geschirr spülen und abtrocknen, und mal die ... die Küche sauber machen, meine Mutter erwartet das von mir, weil sie hat selbst schon genug zu tun. Aber es hält sich noch in Grenzen.

[Eva] Also, ich also, meine Oma ist vor kurzem gestorben und das heißt, dass ich jetzt den Haushalt alleine führen muss, weil ich wohne noch mit meinem Vater zusammen, und ich muss praktisch alles machen. Ich muss Wäsche waschen, ich muss Teller abwischen, ich muss abtrocknen, Staub saugen. Und irgendwann nervt das auch, aber, na ja, man muss es halt machen.

[Karl] Ja, ich mache gar nichts, meine Mutter macht alles für mich, und ich habe nichts zu tun, ist okay.

[Tina] Ja, Haushalt, abwaschen, sprich Staub saugen, einkaufen, Wäsche waschen, Fenster putzen. Ich helf meiner Mutter.

[Ingo] Ja, aufräumen, dann halt mein Zimmer sauber halten, das ist so das Weiteste, dass es da nicht aussieht wie im Urwald.

Videoclips: Werbung

Und wie immer an dieser Stelle: Werbung aus Deutschland

Werbung 1
Oh Köstlichkeiten, euch zu sehen, kaum kann mein Gaumen euch widerstehen. Wild schlägt mein Herz für Pfirsich Melba, bei Sahnerollen schmelz ich hin. Nach Apfelstrudel, Apfelkuchen, Apfeltorte steht mein Sinn. Die Kirsche, rot und reif, und rund.

Kapitel 12 cont.

Tja, Coppenrath und Wiese, die beliebteste Konditorei Deutschlands.

Was hält mich länger noch zurück? Ich will ein großes kleines Stück.

Coppenrath und Wiese, immer allererste Sahne.

Coppenrath und Wiese.

Werbung 2
Es hat damit angefangen, dass wir die besten Torten am Ort gebacken haben. Das hat dazu geführt, dass immer mehr Leute an immer mehr Orten unsere Torten haben wollten. Darum gibt es sie bei Ihrem Kaufmann tiefgekühlt. Und darum schmecken sie immer noch so sahnig frisch wie von der besten Konditorei am Ort. Coppenrath und Wiese — immer allererste Sahne.

Werbung 3
Tengelmann und Kaisers: Haushalt live. Aktuelles und Tips rund um den Haushalt. Heute zum Thema: Vegetarisch grillen.

Es muss nicht immer Kotelett sein, grillen Sie doch mal vegetarisch. Sie glauben gar nicht, wie das schmeckt. Also, nichts wie hin zu Tengelmann und Kaisers. Tomaten, Kartoffeln, Auberginen, Austernpilze, Paprika, Mais und Obst. Die Bananen haben ihre ganz besondere Geschmacksnote, wenn sie vom Grill kommen. Dazu gehören natürlich die richtigen Soßen und Dips. Mit Cremor 0,2%, dem Cremequark der Magerstufe, lassen sich da ganz leicht herrliche Dips zubereiten, indem sie frische Kräuter und Gewürze dazugeben. Zum natürlichen Grillgut passt Vi-Thai von Danone, die leckere und herrlich cremige Komposition aus Magermilch, Frucht und Soja in verschiedenen Sorten. Und jetzt noch ein Tip, an den man oftmals gar nicht denkt: Die beliebten Folienkartoffeln brauchen circa 45 Minuten Garzeit. Also früh genug auf den Grill geben, wenn alles gleichzeitig fertig werden soll. Also, dann tschüs, bis nächsten Dienstag bei Haushalt live, wenn's um's Thema Energiespender geht.

Werbung 4
Hallo, hier ist wieder Frosta mit der feinen Mahlzeit. Ihr wisst doch, da sind nur feine Sachen drin: Huhn, Pilze, Bambus. Also, André Kemper hat's so gut geschmeckt, er hat uns diesen Film geschickt:

Wenn meine Enkel kommen, muss ich ihnen immer Frosta machen, weil's ihnen so gut schmeckt. Und das ist, weißt du eigentlich, dass das morgen früh im Fernsehen ist? Ne? Frosta ist für alle da!

Werbung 5
Hallo Gartenfreunde! Naturgemäß gärtnern mit Neudorff macht Spaß! Zum Beispiel kompostieren mit System. Holziges wird zunächst im Bio-Shredder zerkleinert, dann mit Rasenschnitt vermischt, und mit Radivit aktiviert. Im Thermo-Komposter kommt es zur raschen Erwärmung und gleichmäßigen Umsetzung. Und schon nach 6-8 Wochen ist wertvoller Mulch-Kompost entstanden. Was meinen Sie, wie gut Ihre Pflanzen damit wachsen. Wenn Sie mehr darüber erfahren wollen, holen Sie sich im Gartenfachhandel Neudorffs Bio-Fibel. Kostenlos!

Answer Key

Location Opener 1 Activity Master

1. 1 die Glienicker Brücke
    3 die Fußgängerzone
    2 der Alte Markt
    7 das Chinesische Teehaus
    4 das Brandenburger Tor
    9 Schloss Cecilienhof
    8 Babelsberger Schloss
    5 das Holländische Viertel
    6 Schloss Sanssouci
2. 1. c   4. e
    2. a   5. b
    3. f   6. d

Chapter 1 Activity Master 1

1. 1. Klasse! Super!
    2. neu
    3. Aus
    4. Ja, klar!
    5. heißt
2. 1. stimmt
    2. stimmt nicht (Holger)
    3. stimmt nicht (Holger)
    4. stimmt nicht (Ahmet)
    5. stimmt
3. Christina - Moped
    Sonja - U-Bahn, Fahrrad
    Sandra - Bus, Fahrrad, Auto
    Johannes - Fahrrad
    Tim - Moped

Chapter 1 Activity Masters 2–3

1. Numbers will vary.
2. Bietigheim is a small city (suburb of Stuttgart) and does not have its own subway system. It is not close enough to be connected to the Stuttgart subway system.
3. Herr Gärtner
4. Steffi, Tara, Ahmet, Holger
5. Güle Güle
6. Answers will vary. Examples: Guten Tag! Ich heiße ..., Wie heißt du? Ich komme aus ...
7. Answers will vary.
8. 1. a
    2. c
    3. b

9. c
10. b
11. c
12. Answers will vary.

Chapter 2 Activity Master 1

1. Fußball spielen, schwimmen, Ski laufen, Briefmarken sammeln, Musik hören, Gitarre spielen
2. Karten spielen, Tennis spielen
3.–7. Answers will vary.
8. 1. c
    2. b
    3. d
    4. e
    5. a
9. **a., b.** Answers will vary.

Chapter 2 Activity Masters 2–3

1., 2. Activities mentioned: basteln, tanzen, Saxophon spielen, Tennis, schwimmen, Fernseh gucken, Eis laufen, Rollschuh fahren, faulenzen, Musik hören, Handball spielen, Keyboard spielen, Freunde treffen, Fitnesstraining, Fahrrad fahren, ins Kino gehen, Computer, Eis essen, mit Freunden quatschen, ins Konzert gehen, Basketball/Tischtennis spielen, Squash spielen, sammeln
3., 4. Answers will vary.
5. Items to be checked: a, c, d, f
6. Boris Becker
7. He likes Tara—and Tara likes tennis!
8. He can play well; he likes to play with Tara and Steffi.
9. Answers will vary. Examples: schwimmen, joggen, Fitnesstraining, Rasen mähen
10. Nesfit - bicycle
    Isostar - volleyball
    Cebion plus Magnesium - saxophone
11. schwimmen, relaxen, im Wasser spielen
12. dance, golf, kayaking, hang-gliding, rock climbing
13. Answers will vary.

German 1 Komm mit!   Video Guide

Chapter 3 Activity Master 1

1. 1. mit dem Moped
    2. eine Cola
    3. ein Stück Kuchen
2. 1. Tara
    2. He met (and liked) Tara at school. He though Tara was Jens's girlfriend.
    3. He came to the wrong conclusion about Tara.
3. Dominick - Pinneberg
    Jasmin - Reichenau-Schule, Türkei
    Johanna - Hamburg
    Thomas - Reichenau-Schule, Italien
    Ingo - Gustav-Falke-Straße

Chapter 3 Activity Masters 2-3

1. Answers will vary.
2. Answers will vary.
3. 1. Deutsch, Mathe
    2. rotbraune Haare, dunkle Augen
    3. Handan
4. 1. Answers will vary.
    2. Answers will vary.
5. 1. e
    2. c
    3. b
    4. f
    5. a
    6. d
6. 1. d
    2. b or a [both possible]
    3. a
    4. c

Location Opener 2 Activity Master

1. 1. Elbe
    2. Mittwoch u. Freitag
    3. das Reepschläger Haus, der Anker, der Roland
    4. Mai bis September
2. 1. c
    2. a
    3. e
    4. d
    5. b

3. 1. a, b
    2. go sailing, go swimming, enjoy the outdoors
    4. Answers will vary.

Chapter 4 Activity Master 1

1. 1. Vier
    2. 16 Euro
    3. 10 Euro
    4. Julia
    5. der Taschenrechner
2. 1. Lars
    2. Julia
    3. die Verkäuferin
    4. Lars
    5. Julia
    6. Lars
3. Jasmin likes: Arbeitslehre, Sport, Englisch; does not like: Kunst, Mathe, Physik
    Michael likes: Mathe, Physik, Kunst; does not like: Chemie
    Dirk likes: Englisch, Spanisch, Französisch
    Lugana likes: Englisch, Deutsch
    Björn likes: Physik, Mathematik, Informatik

Chapter 4 Activity Masters 2-3

1. Answers will vary.
2. Lieblingsfächer: all subjects listed except Musik, Religion
    Courses not liked: Biologie, Chemie, Deutsch, Englisch, Geschichte, Mathe, Physik
3. Answers will vary.
4. Answers will vary.
5. 1. Er hat keine Batterien.
    2. 4
    3. Julia
    4. zwei Bleistifte, drei Hefte, einen Radiergummi, ein Wörterbuch, einen Kuli, sechs Farbstifte
    5. morgen
6. She gives him € 7,60 (4 for calculator, 3.60 for batteries)
7., 8., and 9.: Answers will vary.

Chapter 5   Activity Master 1

1. 1. b
   2. c
   3. c
   4. d
2. Answers will vary.
3. Answers will vary.
4. Sandra: blau, weiß; Alexandra: blau, Pastellfarben; Melina: blau, apricot, rot, lila; Iwan: schwarz
5. Answers will vary.

Chapter 5   Activity Masters 2–3

1. Bluse (once)
   Jacke (once)
   Jeans (11 times); blue, black
   Docks (once)
   Hose (once)
   eine kurze Hose (twice)
   Pulli (once)
   Rock (once)
   T-Shirt (8 times); black
   Turnschuhe (once)
   Sandalen (once)
   Dirndlkleider (once)
2. Answers will vary. Examples: Jeans, Jacke, T-Shirt
3. Answers will vary. (Mostly it is the comfortable clothes, such as jeans, docks, and T-shirts that seem to have caught on the most among German young people.)
4. 1. b
   2. b
5. She has seen the boys with their "copy-cat" T-shirts.
6. She is upset, a little angry.
7. gemein; it means "mean, rude"
8. to get back at her for laughing at his T-shirt
9. 1. stimmt
   2. stimmt nicht
   3. stimmt nicht: mit Perwoll gewaschen
10., 11. Answers will vary.

Chapter 6   Activity Master 1

1. 4:30
2. 1. d
   2. a
   3. c.
   4. b
3. 1. b
   2. b
   3. Answers will vary.
4. 1. c
   2. b
   3. d
   4. a

Chapter 6   Activity Masters 2–3

1. Number of times mentioned:
   Hausaufgaben: 5
   Sport: 8
   Musik: 6
   mit Freunden etwas tun: 7
   in eine Disco gehen/tanzen: 4
   ins Kino gehen: 3
   ins Theater gehen: 2
   Klavier spielen: 1
   Tennis spielen: 2
   Fahrrad fahren: 2
   schwimmen: 2
   reiten: 1
2. Sport, Musik, mit Freunden etwas tun
3. Answers will vary.
4. 1. stimmt nicht (Der Fleck geht wahrscheinlich raus.)
   2. stimmt
   3. stimmt nicht (Mineralwasser)
   4. stimmt
   5. stimmt nicht (Sie findet, er sieht gut aus.)
   6. stimmt nicht (Er gibt ihr Blumen.)
   7. stimmt nicht (Sie ist nicht mehr sauer.)
5. apologized, gave her flowers; yes; she smiled, said "Jetzt bin ich nicht mehr sauer."
6. Order: Junghans, Wagner, Sacher, Überkinger
7. 1. c
   2. d
   3. a
   4. b

ANSWER KEY

German 1 Komm mit!

8. 1. watches with ideas
    2. once Wagner, always Wagner
    3. Sacher — the beginning of a great passion.
    4. Überkinger: feel the power of the minerals!
9. Answers will vary.

Location Opener 3 Activity Master

1. 1. alt
    2. zwei
    3. Geschichte
    4. 14.-18. Jahrhundert
    5. bayrischen Kurfürsten und Prinzen
    6. in München
2. 1. b
    2. d
    3. a
    4. c
3. Answers will vary.
4. 1. Bayern
    2. ein Buch lesen, essen, auf Freunde warten
    3. der Dom, das Münchner Kindl
    4. der älteste Lebensmittelmarkt in München

Chapter 7 Activity Master 1

1. a. Claudia
    b. Flori and Markus
    c. Mara
2. 1. to the English Garden
    2. She has chores to do at home.
    3. Flori
    4. vacuuming (Staub saugen)
    5. no; they have to find the cat.
3. 1. b
    2. a
    3. c

Chapter 7 Activity Masters 2-3

1. Answers will vary.
2. 1. die Luft verpesten
    2. Abfall
    3. kompostiert
    4. umweltfreundliche
    5. sparen
    6. Tonne

3. 1. stimmt nicht (Er isst kein Katzenfutter — Kuchen)
    2. stimmt
    3. stimmt nicht (Claudia)
    4. stimmt nicht (Mara)
    5. stimmt nicht (Florian — Markus)
    6. stimmt
4. 1. Winter
    2. Leipzig
    3. Palma de Mallorca, Athen
5. 1. a
    2. d
    3. b
    4. e
    5. c
6. Answers will vary.

Chapter 8 Activity Master 1

1. 1, 2, 4, 5, 7
2. 1. b
    2. a
    3. b
    4. a
3. Answers will vary.
4. 1. Brigitte
    2. Silvana
    3. Iwan
    4. Sandra

Chapter 8 Activity Masters 2-3

1. 1. Nachhilfe
    2. Rechtschreibung
    3. Nachbarschaft
    4. Gesellschaft, langweilig
    5. Kinderkirche, unregelmäßig
2. b
3. ein Kilo Tomaten; eine Gurke; ein Salat; sechs Pfirsiche
4. lecker, saftig
5. 1. e
    2. b
    3. g
    4. a
    5. d
    6. c
    7. f

6. 1. d
   2. f
   3. c
   4. a
   5. g
   6. e
   7. b
7. Answers will vary.

Chapter 9 Activity Master 1

1. 1. stimmt nicht (Säfte)
   2. stimmt
   3. stimmt nicht (Wisconsin)
   4. stimmt nicht (Leberkäs)
   5. stimmt
   6. stimmt nicht (Sie zeigen den Amerikanern die Stadt.)
2. Answers will vary. Examples: immer geradeaus bis zur Ampel, nach rechts, nach links
3. Answers will vary. Example: Geh zuerst nach rechts in die Schwanthalerstraße bis zur Ecke. Dann geh nach rechts in the Schillerstraße. An der zweiten Straße geh nach links, dann geradeaus bis zur Sendlingerstraße. Geh nach links, dann geradeaus. An der Neuhauser-Kaufingerstraße geh nach rechts. Geh immer geradeaus, dann siehst du das Hofbräuhaus auf der linken Seite.
4. Answers will vary.
5. 1. Rosi
   2. Uli
   3. Melina

Chapter 9 Activity Masters 2–3

1. Answers will vary.
2. Answers will vary.
3. mentioned one time: Eis, Schnitzel, Linseneintopf, Eierkuchen, Kaiserschmarren, Gemüse, Cheeseburger, Tortellini, Ravioli, Pommes, Speckknödel, Rouladen mit Klößen, Kohlrouladen; mentioned twice: Gulasch, Hamburger, Knödel, Lasagne; mentioned three times: Spätzle, Salat, Wurst; mentioned six times: Pizza, Spaghetti

4. nationalities mentioned: österreichisch, amerikanisch, italienisch, deutsch, chinesisch, asiatisch, spanisch, indonesisch, mexikanisch, türkisch, griechisch
5., 6., 7. Answers will vary.
8. essen, lesen, miteinander sprechen, auf Freunde warten
9. 1. c
   2. e
   3. d
   4. a
   5. f
   6. h
   7. b
   8. g
10. Answers will vary. Examples: buy stamps, mail letters, mail and pick up packages.
11. fährt ein Auto, spielt mit einem Computer, spielt Schach
12. Fisch essen
13. mail letters, maintain a savings account
14. banking in German post office

Location Opener 4 Activity Master

1. 1. 25
   2. mittelalterliche
   3. Bietigheim
   4. eine Fußgängerzone
   5. 17. Jahrhundert
   6. Samstag
   7. Gasse
2. 1. c
   2. b
   3. d
   4. a
3. Answers will vary.

Chapter 10 Activity Master 1

1. activities mentioned: diskutieren, joggen, Karten spielen, kegeln, lachen, lesen, musizieren, radeln, Schach spielen, segeln, singen, Skateboard fahren, traurig sein, warten
2. 1. c
   2. c
   3. d
   4. a

5. a
6. b
Answers will vary. Possible sentences: Martin und Sandra schauen die Kassetten an. Thomas hört die „Toten Hosen" an. Andreas und Nicole warten auf ihre Freunde. Sabine liest ein Buch.
3. b
4. 1. Silke
   2. Rosi
   3. Silvana
   4. Tim

Chapter 10 Activity Masters 2–3

1. cultural events:
   Opern: 2
   Kinos: 3
   Theateraufführungen: 8
   Konzerte: 1
   Ballette: 1
   Ausstellungen: 3
   Museen: 2
2. Answers will vary.
3. 1. Geld
   2. Freundin
   3. Freund
   4. krank
   5. Bank
   6. ehrlich
   7. Millionär
   8. Konto
4., 5., 6.: Answers will vary.

Chapter 11 Activity Master 1

1. 1. b (Martin)
   2. b (Kassette)
   3. a
   4. b (eine Karte)
2. Answers will vary.
3. 1. b
   2. c
   3. d
   4. a

Chapter 11 Activity Masters 2–3

1. items mentioned as gifts: Bild, Bücher, CDs, Gutscheine, Kassetten, Lego™, T-Shirt
2. Answers will vary.
3. 1. Sommer
   2. August
   3. nie
   4. elften August
   5. achtzehnten August
4. His birthday party is planned for Saturday, but his birthday is not until August.
5. 1. a
   2. b, c, d, f
   3. e, h
6., 7., 8.: Answers will vary.

Chapter 12 Activity Master 1

1. 1. b, d
   2. c
   3. a
   4. b, d, e
2., 3. Answers will vary.
4. 1. h, d, f, i
   2. g, d, b
   3. a, b, d, c
   4. c, d, a, e

Chapter 12 Activity Masters 2–3

1. Household chores mentioned:
   abwaschen: 4
   den Rasen mähen: 3
   den Müll rausbringen: 2
   den Geschirrspüler ausräumen: 4
   die Küche wischen: 3
   Fenster putzen: 1
   Mülleimer runterbringen: 1
   Staub saugen: 5
   Toilette sauber machen: 1
   Wäsche aufhängen: 2
   Zimmer aufräumen: 4
   also mentioned: Treppe putzen, im Garten arbeiten, einkaufen
2. Answers will vary.
3. Beverages mentioned: Erdbeerbowle, Limo, Orangensaft
   Foods mentioned: Brezeln, Gurkensalat, Kartoffelsalat, Krautsalat, Kuchen, Tomatensalat, Wurstbrote
4. Answers will vary.
5. 1. d
   2. b
   3. e
   4. c
   5. a
6., 7., 8.: Answers will vary.